SHOE TIME

SHOE TIME

by Aimee Liu and Meg Rottman

TIMBRE BOOKS

Arbor House • New York

Manufactured in the United States of America

10 9 8 7 6 5 4 3 2 1

Library of Congress Cataloging in Publication Data

Liu, Aimee.
Shoe time!

(Timbre books)
1. Shoes—Social aspects. 2. Shoes—Psychological
aspects. 3. Shoes—History. 4. Shoe industry—
History. I. Rottman, Meg. II. Title. III. Series.
GT2130.L58 1986   391'.413   85-18701
ISBN: 0-87795-737-1 (pbk.)

Certain products, mentioned throughout this book, are protected under
registered brand names or trademarks. These include but are not limited to
the following: Adidas®, Andrew Geller®, Asics Tiger®, Bata®, Bernardo®,
Bill Blass®, Birkenstock®, Buster Brown®, Coca-Cola®, Converse®, Etonic®,
Evan Picone®, Famolare®, Gatorade®, Gloria Vanderbilt®, Hang Ten®, Hush
Puppies®, IBM®, Jacques Cohen®, Kaepa®, Keds®, L. A. Gear™, Levi's®, Liz
Claiborne®, Monopoly®, Nike®, Oomphies®, Phylon™, Polly Bergen™,
Puma®, Sperry Topsider®, Tootsie Roll®, Trivial Pursuit®, Velcro®

To
Marty, Daniel, and Graham
and
Jeff, Molly, and Adam

CONTENTS

SHOES, GLORIOUS SHOES!

An Introduction

- Today's average American family of three purchases fourteen pairs of shoes every year.
- According to psychologists, shoe and foot fetishes are the most common forms of sexual fetishism in Western society.
- Archaeologists have dug up evidence of shoemaking as early as 10,000 B.C.
- You spend eighteen out of every twenty-four hours in shoes of one form or another.
- In your lifetime you'll walk the equivalent of three to four times around the earth, or between 70,000 and 115,000 miles.
- The human foot contains 26 bones, 19 muscles, and 120 ligaments, almost the same number as in the hand. The 52 bones in your two feet make up about one fourth of all the bones in your body.
- You can tell whether a person is left-handed or right-handed by checking the wear on his or her shoes. Since people bear down harder on the dominant side, the sole on that side will be worn down more than the other side.
- The human foot doesn't fully straighten out until age five or six. The foot doesn't completely finish growing until about age twenty.

- Each day, the average person puts nearly 1,000 tons of pressure on the feet, and takes 8,000 to 10,000 steps.
- Soccer players take as many as 10,000 steps in a single game, their feet absorbing a cumulative total pressure of more than 1,000 tons of pressure per player. A 100-pound ballerina lands from a *grand jeté* with a force of nearly a quarter ton.
- Approximately 87 percent of the American population, nearly 200 million people, have foot problems of some kind. Women have four times as much foot trouble as men.
- Approximately 63 percent of Americans think it's normal for feet to hurt.
- Blisters, calluses, and corns are the most common foot problems.
- Your feet may swell as much as 5 percent in an average day.
- 45 percent of women and 20 percent of men wear shoes that hurt in order to look fashionable; 22 percent of women claim that they'd continue wearing high heels even if they knew the shoes were damaging their feet.
- Only 13 percent of Americans view their feet as ugly. The rest think their feet are attractive.
- Nearly one fourth of all Americans between the ages eighteen and twenty-four say they go barefoot most of the time.
- There are approximately 7,500 practicing podiatrists in this country. They each earn more than $42,000 per year. Together they handle more than 32 million office visits each year.
- People whose feet hurt spend over $200 million each year on over-the-counter remedies for aching feet.
- Americans spend almost $7 billion a year on footwear, plus another $250 million on shoes for running.

Kids wear them. Grandmothers wear them. Even astronauts in space wear them. Isn't it about time we brought shoes out of the closet and took a closer look at them? No other item in your wardrobe takes as much of a beating as your shoes, nor does any other piece of clothing have as much of an impact on your health, comfort, *and* attitude.

Shoes are the unsung heroes of the fashion world. You can deck yourself out in a million-dollar ensemble, but you'll never come up to *Vogue* standards if your shoes clash with your outfit. Some of the world's most innovative designers have been lured to the artistry—and potential profit—involved in maintaining the subtle but critical importance of shoes as a fashion ingredient. The result is a constant race among designers to provide us all with the "perfect" shoes for every occasion. This, in turn, has spawned a multimillion-dollar footwear industry that encompasses manufacturers, laborers, and retailers on every continent.

But you don't have to be in the footwear industry to love shoes. You don't have to be a foot or shoe fetishist. You don't even have to wear shoes, though that may help. All you really need is an eye for style and a taste for trivia. We'll supply the rest. Read on.

1

SHOES AS ART

Shoes of the Stars

Magic Shoes and Movie Shoes

Dorothy's Ruby Slippers

The most famous of all movie shoes are the ruby slippers worn by Judy Garland in the 1939 version of *The Wizard of Oz*. The shoes were red patent leather, with sequins that shimmered magically throughout the movie. Just as the slippers were Dorothy's ticket to fantasy, they became a symbol of wonder and childhood for millions of Americans as soon as the film was released.

There were actually six pairs of ruby slippers during the filming of *Oz*. The producer Mervyn LeRoy estimated that between five or ten pairs were produced as backups in case the originals were damaged by tripping, falling, scratching, or other calamities. But only one pair surfaced when MGM's Wardrobe Department was cleaned out in preparation for the studio's multimillion-dollar auction in 1970.

The slippers were wrapped in a towel and buried in a bin in the basement. They were covered with dust, and sequins were missing, but the shoes were restored to mint condition in time for the auction. MGM was hoping the proceeds from the auction would make a sizable contribution toward the building of the $125 million MGM Grand Hotel in Las Vegas. Studio executives didn't overlook the profit potential of Dorothy's ruby slippers. They were the most valuable clothing item on the lot, and arguably the most valuable shoes in the world.

The auction lasted for eighteen days, beginning on May 3, 1970. For a week beforehand the slippers were displayed along with the other merchandise for inspection by prospective bidders. Unlike the other items for sale, the slippers were not identified. They didn't need to be. They sat in a glass case and gleamed in the overhead light. Hundreds gathered around to look at them.

The slippers were auctioned, along with the Cowardly Lion's costume and Clark Gable's "good luck" trenchcoat, at 8 P.M. on Sunday, May 17. The audience was guessing the shoes would bring up to $9,000. Debbie Reynolds claimed she would bid $5,000 to purchase the slippers for a museum of Hollywood artifacts that she was attempting to establish. Martin Lotz, the mayor of Culver City, home of MGM, was willing to spend $7,500, which he'd received in pledges in order to buy the shoes for "the little children" of Culver City. Harry Robbins, the president of a company called Carolina Caribbean, was prepared to spend $11,000 in order to have the shoes for his company's theme park, The Land of Oz.

In the 46 seconds it took to auction the shoes, Debbie Reynolds didn't even get her bid in. Mayor Lotz offered $7,000, then quit. Robbins's bid was immediately outstripped. The winning price of $15,000 was bid by a young lawyer acting as proxy for an unidentified client. The media never did discover the identity of the slippers' new owner, nor his motive for paying such an exorbitant sum for his prize. The lawyer, Richard Wonder, contacted his client in 1975 to ask if he'd consent to a telephone interview with a reporter. The request was denied.

As for the other sets of ruby slippers, one pair belonging to Judy Garland's stand-in was given away in a contest soon after the movie was released. One pair is now on display, right across from Archie Bunker's chair, at the Smithsonian Institution's Museum of American History in Washington, D.C. Two pairs of the slippers disappeared from the MGM wardrobe department well before the auction, and in 1974 one of these was offered to Debbie Reynolds for her fledgling museum.

A fifth pair of red-sequined, leather-lined slippers also bearing Judy Garland's name inside was purchased in 1974 by Ted Smith, a former clown for Barnum & Bailey Circus. Smith paid an undisclosed amount to an unidentified man who had worked in the MGM wardrobe department. Smith wanted the slippers for his San Francisco antique memorabilia store, Humpty Dumpty & Sons.

Ten years later, Smith claimed that the value of *his* ruby slippers had risen to $20,000, considerably more than the MGM auction bid by the phantom buyer. If Smith's estimate is correct it's no wonder that the shoes were the object of a robbery at Humpty Dumpty and Sons in late 1983. Two men with a gun entered the store and demanded that the slippers be placed in a cardboard box. Perhaps the thieves didn't know there were other ruby slippers in the world, or perhaps they didn't care. Almost five decades after *The Wizard of Oz* was made, the mystique of the magic slippers lives on.

Ginger Rogers

Ginger Rogers has danced her way through many pairs of shoes in her life, but the most demanding of all her movies was *Top Hat* (1935). Among the memorabilia from that film many of the dresses remain but none of the shoes. The actress had a ready explanation for this: "We did so much dancing and rehearsing that the shoes would disintegrate on my feet." The studio costume department delivered pair after pair, with the glue still wet. Unfortunately, the cast was working under such a grueling production schedule that they couldn't wait for the shoes to dry. According to Ginger Rogers, "Dancing in wet pumps is an art form in itself."

Stand-ins for the Stars

Ginger Rogers's longtime partner, Fred Astaire, had help wearing down his shoes. He called on a special stand-in with his shoe size to break in each new pair of dancing shoes for him. He didn't invent this practice, however. Before Astaire, the great American showman George M. Cohan and French emperor Napoleon Bonaparte also had servants break in their shoes for them.

Teny Lama

It's a boot! It's a sneaker! No, it's a Teny Lama, the combination cowboy boot and tennis shoe first designed as a joke by the Tony Lama boot company in 1984. The game-show host Bob Eubanks wore the improved footgear on the air and started a mini-trend among viewers and colleagues. Other celebrity Teny Lama customers include the race-car driver A. J. Foyt and his crew, the singer Willie Nelson and his band, and the Redskin running back John Riggins.

Florenz Ziegfeld

The master of 1920s showmanship used high heels as a valuable tool in auditioning dancers for his extravaganzas. For their audition, young women were requested to walk in heels behind a white screen so that Ziegfeld could examine their gait in silhouette: Before I see their faces, I want to see how they walk. There's more sex in a walk than in a face or even in a figure."

Queen Elizabeth II of England

The queen's daily schedule includes hours of standing in reception lines, walking officially through foreign nations, and marching prominently in royal processions. At one official gathering she shook hands with 1,574 guests and stood for over 2 hours. She's expected to maintain grace and dignity at all times and to never show fatigue. Aching feet would seriously jeopardize her performance, and as a result she wears only one style of shoe—a 2-inch pump that's comfortable rather than trendy.

Lobb of St. James has been shoemaker to her Royal Highness since 1946. The queen's shoes are handmade personally by Edward Rayne. He provides her with plain black or white calfskin court shoes for daytime and gold or silver kidskin slippers for evening. Though the designs are simple, these shoes are among the most expensive in the world.

Princess Diana's Wedding Slippers

The date was July 29, 1981, the place, St. Paul's Cathedral in London. Millions all over the world watched that day as Lady Diana Spencer stepped regally down the aisle to marry the world's most eligible bachelor, Prince Charles of England. But not more than a handful could have seen the elegant slippers hidden under the bride's trailing wedding gown until she knelt, revealing the detailed soles. The new princess's footwear was a masterpiece of design, executed by Clive Shilton, one of England's most exclusive and expensive young shoe designers.

The details of the wedding were shrouded in secrecy for months before the nuptials. The shoes were no exception. Shilton, like the designers working on the rest of the bridal outfit, was sworn to secrecy about his plans. He and his partner, Julie Smith, crafted the slippers by hand in their Covent Garden shop with the help of just nine assistants.

One critical concern for the shoemakers was Lady Di's comfort and grace. Even though Lady Di had to pull some 20-odd yards of wedding-gown train down the aisle, this wedding could not afford a stumble or fall. To avoid disaster, Shilton covered the slippers' soles with suede and edged them in smooth gold. Another worry for the royal family was Diana's height. At 5'10", it wouldn't take much of a heel to lift the new princess above the head of her prince. Shilton discreetly solved the problem with tiny but elegant fluted heels.

The royal wedding slipper design also called for 134 pearls and 542 mother-of-pearl sequins. The shoes were covered with ivory silk top-stitched in a diamond pattern. On the toes were flat hearts and lace rosettes with ruffled borders. Under the arch of each slipper was an intricate hand-painted gold-leaf motif of hearts, flowers, and leaves with the initials "C" and "D." Each shoe had its own satin sac, and for the pair there was a royal-blue velvet sac with matching satin lining. To complete the package, the drawstring on the outer sac ended with blue pleated satin flowers with pearl stamens.

For safety's sake, an identical pair of shoes was made, and on the wedding day a member of the royal staff carried *this* pair in case anything went wrong with the originals.

Shilton's shoes normally cost upward of $220, but he refused to divulge either the expense of the royal slippers or the size of the royal bride's feet. (The press later discovered that her size is 9½.) After the wedding, the slippers went on a round-the-world tour so that the public finally could glimpse the historic shoes. Once home again in Britain, the slippers became royal artifacts, perhaps never to be worn again.

Emperor Hirohito of Japan
In keeping with Japanese tradition, Hirohito wore the platform sandals called *geta* for his coronation in 1926. But the height of his *geta* was quite beyond tradition—his sandals lifted him a full foot off the ground.

Erma Bombeck
Writer Erma Bombeck may not be known for her own shoes, but she has very definite opinions about *other* women's shoes and why they buy them.

First of all style. It very definitely comes before comfort, according to Bombeck. In fact, the *lack* of comfort may be the key indicator of fashion. "If they don't cause pain, then they don't have style." The true sign of a fashionable shoe for Bombeck is the 8-inch heel. These heels have multiple purposes, such as adding height, causing blisters, and shedding those 20 extra pounds that *refuse* to come off through diet.

Second, the issue of quantity. Bombeck's woman must have at least fifteen to twenty pairs. At least one pair must have multiple straps to make the ankle look thinner, and a couple of pairs should be two sizes too small, in case other women at parties want to compare shoe sizes. Six or seven pairs should be purchased to match specific outfits so the owner can fit in with the Junior League set. Every footwear wardrobe should also include sports shoes, especially if the woman is *not* athletic. These shoes are great for wearing to the grocery store, and wearing them will make others *think* you're athletic. Perhaps the most important athletic shoes of all are Bombeck's driving shoes. These slip over the gas pedal and can be left in the front seat between car trips.

Bombeck says many men cannot understand why women need so many shoes. But then, these same men can't possibly understand why women need company to go to the powder room.

Neil Armstrong

On July 20, 1969, the astronaut Neil Armstrong became the first man to set foot on the moon. Everyone remembers his proclamation: "That's one small step for man, one giant leap for mankind." But how many people remember his micrometeroid boots?

Armstrong's footwear for that historic visit was constructed like a thermos bottle. The outer surface was blue and white fire- and abrasion-resistant fabric. The insulation consisted of alternate layers of aluminized material and low-heat-conducting spacer fabric. The inside was lined with a layer of rubber-coated nylon, and the soles were made of thick corrugated silicone rubber, which wrapped over the toes and heels. The boot wrapped snugly around the ankle and snapped tight. A strap buckled over the instep.

Unfortunately, the historic boots were jettisoned away in the lunar module in order to prevent contamination when the astronauts returned to earth. The boots on display in science museums are only copies.

Celebrity Shoe Collections
Footstyles of the Rich and Famous

Celebrities have several excuses for becoming shoe lovers: (1) They tend to have enough money to buy *truly wonderful* shoes, (2) they have endless "occasions" to which they need to wear many different kinds of shoes, and (3) it's important to their careers to cultivate their own fashion looks and to coordinate their wardrobes from head to toe. With all these motivating factors, it's not surprising that many stars are avid shoe collectors. Here's a glimpse into the closets of just a few of celebrity footwear fans.*

*Shoe wardrobe sizes are approximate.

ANN-MARGRET 300 pairs
"I own 300 pairs of shoes; I've saved them since 1961. I guess I thought if I held onto them long enough they'd come back into style." *(Harper's Bazaar)*

PRISCILLA BARNES *(formerly of the TV series Three's Company)*
150 pairs

CANDICE BERGEN
"In the country, I dress like a bag lady—sweatshirts and overalls and Wellingtons. In Paris [Candice Bergen lives in France] I'm so acutely aware of not being able to put things together with the style French women have I just dress very American—khakis and sneakers—and say, 'to hell with it.'" *(Harper's Bazaar)*

POLLY BERGEN 300+ pairs
Married to the Dori Shoe Company president, Jeff Enderwelt, Polly Bergen has ready access to the shoe market, and she takes advantage of it. She'll buy five to eight pairs at a time. "I keep clothes and shoes for a long time and have used my own wardrobe in acting work, so the extra room in my house is my closet. I have clothes and shoes from 30 years ago. I have open racks for shoes." Her love for footwear prompted her to establish her own line of shoes. The new venture allowed her to share in her husband's business world. It was a source of potential profit. But she also had another motive: "To act you have to be thin. You can be heavy and still make shoes."

KAREN BLACK 60 pairs

DAVID BRENNER
Brenner's favorite shoes are loafers, but not because they're stylish or comfortable. He likes them because of their effect on weight reduction! Brenner's weight-loss formula? Wear loafers while sitting to burn 30 calories. Wear loafers while jogging and burn an extra 40 calories. Wear loafers while watching a Humphrey Bogart movie and burn 50 calories. And wear loafers without doing anything else to burn off 20 calories. (This plan is not recommended for anyone with a legitimate weight problem.)

MORGAN BRITTANY *(Dallas)*   48 pairs of shoes
                                                        15 pairs of boots

LYNDA CARTER *(formerly of the TV series "Wonder Woman")*
                                                        800 pairs of boots

KATE CAPSHAW

Most of actress Kate Capshaw's shoe collection consists of flats. "I bought my first pair of high heels in years for my appearance on Johnny Carson's Show in May of 1984. . . . I feel best in pleated baggy pants, men's Oxford-cloth shirts with maybe a vest and often a tie." *(Harper's Bazaar)*

CHER

The singer-actress once capitalized on her well-known love of shoes by using a giant high-heeled slipper as a prop in a television special. The star made her entrance onstage through a steep slide built into the "shoe's" shank.

LYNDON BAINES JOHNSON

The former President wore size 11 on one foot, 11½ on the other. As a result, he had to have his shoes custom-made. For more than twenty-six years Domenick Dimeola made shoes for LBJ, as well as for Dwight Eisenhower, Harry Truman, John Kennedy, Gerald Ford, Liberace, and Oral Roberts. Dimeola crafts his shoes at a rate of one pair a day. They sell for $450 to $1,200 a pair.

JERRY LEWIS

Like many other celebrities, especially men, it seems, the comedian Jerry Lewis has all his shoes custom-made. To keep his shoes in shape, he has a sizable collection of shoe trees, all purchased from Thom McAn Shoes. During one of Mr. Lewis's stays at the Las Vegas Sahara hotel, he found he'd forgotten to bring trees with him for fourteen pairs of shoes. Thom McAn rushed the necessary shoe trees to him.

ELTON JOHN

One of the few famous male shoe lovers, Elton John feels so strongly about the importance of shoes that he named a hit song in their honor: "Who Wears These Shoes."

LIBERACE

The flamboyant pianist is perhaps better known for his jewels and clothing than for his music. Shoes are as critical an element as any other garment in his wardrobe, which includes more than 500 outfits just for his appearances. His sequined and brocaded costumes are created by the designer Michael Travis. Some of his outfits, including footwear, cost as much as the average American pays for a home.

OLIVIA NEWTON JOHN

The Australian singer sells her shoe collection at her trendy Los Angeles boutique, Koala Blue. The shoes include hand-painted, limited-edition styles. They keep company in the store with stuffed kangaroos, wombats, koala bears, exotic garments, and Australian magazines. The store's name stands for KOrner of Australia, Los Angeles. "Blue" is an Australian term for "friend" or "pal."

DOLLY PARTON

"I spend thousands of dollars on shoes each year." (*Glamour* magazine)

BERNADETTE PETERS   50 pairs

Not much for gala movie-star dressing off the film set, Bernadette Peters prefers casual pants or antique dresses that are "loose fitting, worn with sandals, very 30's, very comfortable." (*Harper's Bazaar*)

NANCY REAGAN

Like most of his well-heeled clients, Mrs. Reagan frequently dresses from head to toe in fashions by her favorite designer, Adolfo. His ensembles include a specific style of footwear: "a pointed toe, high heeled shoe. . . . Very classic and elegant." Beauty, in short, before comfort.

DIONNE WARWICK   400 pairs

RAQUEL WELCH

Once a renowned shoe lover, Raquel Welch has changed her ways in the last few years, after moving from Hollywood to New York, where she became the toast of Broadway as the star of *Woman of the Year*. About her current shoe wardrobe, she reports, "Since my move from California, my interest has shrunk to a minimum. Less time and less space in New York are responsible."

CELEBRITY SHOE SIZES

SHOE SIZE　　　**CELEBRITY**

Politics

SHOE SIZE	CELEBRITY
8	ETHEL BRADLEY (wife of Mayor Tom Bradley, Los Angeles)
10½	WILLIE BROWN (speaker of the house, California)
11–11½	LYNDON BAINES JOHNSON
12½	THOMAS JEFFERSON
12½	WOODROW WILSON
13	GEORGE WASHINGTON
14	WARREN G. HARDING
9½	PRINCESS DIANA

Show Biz

SHOE SIZE	CELEBRITY
4	JUDY GARLAND
4	DEBBIE REYNOLDS
6	RAQUEL WELCH
7	GRETA GARBO
7½	CHRISTINE FERRARE
7½	BING CROSBY
8½	EDWARD G. ROBINSON
9AA	POLLY BERGEN
9	JACK BENNY
9	AL JOLSON
10	HUMPHREY BOGART
10½	FRED ASTAIRE
11	DOUGLAS FAIRBANKS
11	CECIL B. DE MILLE
11	FRANK SINATRA
11½	DEAN MARTIN
12	CARY GRANT

SHOE SIZE	CELEBRITY
12½	JOHN BARRYMORE
12½	CLARK GABLE
13	BOB HOPE
14	GARY COOPER

Fashion

7½	KENZO
10A	WALTER NEWBERGER (footwear designer)
8½	ANDREA PFISTER

Beauty Queens

6½	MISS UNIVERSE 1983—YVONNE RYDING
8	MISS USA 1983—MAI SHANLEY

Sports

3	MARY LOU RETTON
7½	NADIA COMANECI
18	KAREEM ABDUL-JABBAR (Los Angeles Lakers)
18	JAMES DONALDSON (Dallas Mavericks)
19	BOB LANIER (Milwaukee Bucks)

Science

9½	NEIL ARMSTRONG

The Painted Shoe and Such

A Collector's Scrapbook

Portrait of a Shoe Portraitist: Gacci

She may be the only professional shoe portraitist outside of the footwear industry. She doesn't design shoes, and she doesn't work for a shoe company. Gacci simply loves to draw and paint shoes, especially those worn by Broadway stars.

It all began back in the late 1970s, when Gacci was one of millions of young struggling newcomers to Manhattan. Between apprenticing with a film editor and waitressing at Sardi's Restaurant, the famed New York City hangout for Broadway celebrities, Gacci saw every Broadway show she could afford. To amuse herself during slow periods in the editing room she began doodling her colleagues' feet. She then took a second look at the endless caricatures of celebrity faces that hang in Sardi's. It occurred to her that caricatures of performers' *feet* could be just as revealing as facial portraits. So she took a drawing pad along with her to the theater and bought front-row center tickets. "It cost me plenty," she admits, "and all I did was watch the footwear, looking for the perfect pose to sketch that would clearly show the role and, therefore, identify the performer." But it was worth the price. After each show Gacci sent her sketch backstage with a request to take a Polaroid shot of the same pose so that she could do a more elaborate drawing. Jessica Tandy and Hume Cronyn, then appearing in *The Gin Game*, were the first to consent. From then on, it was easy.

The fledgling shoe portraitist got some help from Mr. Sardi, who allowed her to hang her foot works in his restaurant for more than three years, as she says, "giving the faces feet!" The portraits originally sold for $400 apiece (they now cost upward of $1,000), and the display legitimized this new talent in the eyes of both her customers and the stars whose good graces she required.

Gacci has drawn the feet of virtually all the Broadway hits ever since. Each portrait is signed by the subject, who may also add a "footnote." Ken Page of *Ain't Misbehavin'*, for example, ad-libbed some of the lyrics from the song "Your Feet's Too Big" around his portrait. Many of the stars agree with Gacci that the shoes are an integral part of the character they portray. Barnard Hughes, who starred in *Da*, considered his costume shoes a lucky charm. Jack Lemmon broke his shoes in during rehearsals of *Tribute* in order to establish a feel for his role.

The notoriety that came with her shoe portraits also brought Gacci "real work." She began to market her drawings as posters, postcards, and even porcelain coffee mugs. She took her craft to the front windows of chic New York stores, like

Fiorucci and Mario Valentino, where she appeared as a performance artist drawing shoes. Her drawing became an in-
store event at such department stores as Bloomingdale's and B.
Altman. And gradually she attracted the notice of manufacturers, who hired her as a shoe illustrator for ad campaigns.
Gacci is currently the editor of *In Focus,* a publication for the
footwear industry.

The Sculpted Shoe
Like artists in other media, modern sculptors have used the
shoe from time to time as a source for ideas and out-of-the-
ordinary forms. In recent years the shoe has become a favorite
subject for ceramicists and artists who worked with other plia-
ble materials, such as fabric, paper, and leather.

One of the largest shoe sculptures was an installation by the
mixed-media artist Cecilia Brunazzi of the Berkeley Art Center,
California, in 1984. The best description of the piece lies in the
artist's own statement, written for the exhibition's catalog:

> Part of Mother's closet was as drab as camouflage, but in
> the deep recesses of the other portion, unknown to any-
> one but Mother and me, there lay a secret riot of color. A
> celebration of shape. A hymn to line. A reverent eulogy to
> whimsical detail. There lay, disguised in discreet rec-
> tangular boxes, perfectly uniform, an array so vast and
> festive, so luxuriantly varied and discreetly stored, that it
> would have shamed the most acquisitive and discriminat-
> ing connoisseur. There lay . . .
>
> ONE HUNDRED AND TWENTY PAIRS OF SHOES! This
> meant that in a working day, Mother could change her
> shoes every nine and one-half minutes without ever wear-
> ing the same pair twice. The opulence of her excess, the
> folly of her indulgence, her unfettered urge to gratuitous
> accumulation was revealed to me, and only me, as I gained
> sure familiarity with the collection during my furtive in-
> vestigations conducted as soon as I was old enough to be
> left home alone.
>
> As my intimacy with the closet's contents increased dur-
> ing successive visits to her intersanctum, each pair of

shoes acquired the crisp outlines of personality. . . . The matronly but seductive maroon lizard slingbacks, the confident black kid heels with delicate leather pleats fashioned improbably at the toe; the no-nonsense elegant brown alligator pumps; the gay acquamarine canvas sandals she called "espadrilles" reserved exclusively for vacations to tropical climates; the sultry blue satin slippers with feather pompoms naughtily mounting the crest of the arch; the natty summer whites with perforated black cutouts she called "spectators"; the regal navy satins with rhinestone buckles; the pearl grey ostrich hide which murmured sophistication . . . it went on and on.

As time went on, two decidedly curious aspects of her great reserve emerged.

THE FIRST: Considering the expanse of shoes and their cost, there were very few which could be considered practical, although Mother had her pragmatic side. But NO lackluster oxfords for HER, no ties or laces ever marred the delicate curve of her arch, and whereas tennis shoes and orthopedic sandals were standard accoutrements of my childhood wardrobe, no hint of such athleticism sullied the bright aspect of mother's footware aviary where only the most exotic bird lived in shady seclusion.

THE SECOND: This was entirely a sub rosa collection. For whatever fiscal limit my father gave her, she was always compelled to transgress and buy "just one more pair." The store of "one more pairs" was closeted for fear he would view all of her shoes simultaneously. But if she wore them casually, displaying the new acquisitions at judicious intervals, her careful monitoring would prevent him from ever realizing the staggering quantity of her collection, and her budgetary imprudence.

My private childhood knowledge of Mother's varied and rare shoe specimens fostered in me a familiarity and delight in her act of rebellion. But whereas her rebellion was synonymous with the act of acquisition, I have come to interpret the act more amply. I also came to know and carry with me until this day, an appreciation of frivolous beauty at the expense of practicality. And when I revel in a gra-

cious turn of line, a subtle flush of hue, a gratuitously
excessive finial, I smell warm wind redolent of Mother's
distant memory.*

Shoe Ad Artistry

If you think all shoe ads are boring, you haven't been paying
attention to the flowering of shoe ad artistry in this country.
The footwear industry is making an effort to spruce up its
image, and the leader of the pack is Nike—the athletic shoe
and clothing manufacturer based in Beaverton, Oregon.

Nike's ads don't look like ads. They don't feel like ads. They
don't read like ads. They are art first, sales tools second. At
least that's the impression you get from looking at them. In
every one—and they range from street billboards to television
commercials to magazine ads—you have to search for the Nike
logo. In many of the ads that's all you'll find. There are no
heavy-handed or cutesie promotional lines, no lists of stores
where Nikes are sold (they're sold just about everywhere), no
testimonials from satisfied celebrities. There *are* celebrities in
many of the ads, but they appear in picture only. The sub-
liminal message may be, "It's my Nikes that have made me a
champion," but aesthetically the athletes appear only as physically perfect pieces of art.

Nike's advertising campaign attracted the public's and the
media's attention simultaneously around the start of the 1984
summer Olympics in Los Angeles. The innovative L.A.-based ad
agency Chiat/Day handled the account, seeding the town with
Nike billboards featuring front-running Olympic athletes. Nike
had not bought its way in to become an official Olympic sponsor, but everyone in Los Angeles assumed they were a sponsor
because of the prominence of the ads.

Chiat/Day got extra mileage out of Nike's athletic endorsers
in a 60-second TV commercial featuring Randy Newman sing-
ing "I Love L.A." The commercial was a sample of Southern
California street scenes complete with palm trees, beaches,
freeway traffic, and Mann's Chinese Theater. Athletes with
cameo appearances included Carl Lewis, Mary Decker Slaney,

*Reprinted by permission of Cecilia Brunazzi

John McEnroe, and Moses Malone. What was *not* there in prominence was any mention of Nike. If you missed the glimpses of the swoosh trademark or the final tag, "Nike, this summer," you'd think you were watching a rock video. Apparently, not everyone missed the point, however. According to Chiat/Day, Nike's sales rose 30 percent in Los Angeles within six months after the campaign was launched.

Most of the publicity surrounding Nike's trend-setting campaign focused on Chiat/Day as the innovator. Less than a year into its campaign, the firm had won more than twenty awards for its work for Nike. In fact, Chiat/Day is responsible only for Nike's clothing advertising. Advertising for Nike's shoes is handled by Wieden & Kennedy, a firm based in Portland, Oregon. Credit aside, it's virtually impossible for the uninitiated to distinguish between the footwear and clothing ads. Nike's name recognition is all that shines through in either case. And shine it does.

The Shoes of Dance

The ballerina with the torn, bleeding feet; it's an image that came to life in the movie *The Turning Point*. Photographers have created portraits of dancers' feet because they're so emotionally provocative. Among ballerinas themselves, the care and survival of feet is a constant problem.

In ballet the shoe is the most critical piece of equipment. Dancers can go through two or three pairs of slippers in a single performance. They are very particular about fit and quality and look for specific brand names when buying their footwear, especially toe shoes.

Toe, or pointe, shoes are handmade. Their shape is uniform, without distinction as to right or left. Made of wood, glue, nails, and sometimes fiberglass in addition to the fabric upper, these shoes cost about $25 per pair. Professional dancers cannot wear them without first breaking them in. This does not mean wearing them around the house for a couple of days. Rather, dancers brutalize the shoes into submission by pounding them with a hammer until they're soft and smooth. The vamp may be cut lower or the shank shaved to the exact length of the dancer's foot. The shoes are then shellacked until the toe surface is hard. For maximum fit, ballet shoes are often sewn or glued to the dancer's tights. The soles may be sliced to increased flexibility. Ribbons or elastics are added last.

Some of the top ballet shoe manufacturers around the world include

Freed & Gamba Shoe Company *(London)*
Repetto Shoe Company *(Paris)*
Schactner *(Austria)*
Love *(Copenhagen)*
Grand *(exclusive to the Moscow's Bolshoi Ballet)*

The Written Shoe
The Truth About Cinderella, and More

Cinderella Through the Ages

The Cinderella most of us met during childhood was far older than we realized . . . about twenty-four centuries older, in fact. The mysterious lady with the tiny feet was born back in the days of the ancient Greeks. She used the lure of her delicate shoe on kings and princes on several continents before making her debut as the heroine of Disney animation. The tale of Cinderella, her fairy godmother, pumpkin coach, and glass slipper is only the most recent version of a tale whose originals follow.

Cinderella No. 1: Rhodope (c. 600 B.C.)

The first Cinderella was named Rhodope, and she lived in ancient Greece. As a young girl, she worked as a servant in the home of a wealthy man named IADMON. (One of her fellow servants was Aesop, who produced the fables, which have also survived to this day.)

Cinderella was very beautiful and adventurous. She scented her hair with musk oil and stained her lovely feet with henna. Soon she was breaking hearts all over the ancient world. Her first lover was Charaxus, the brother of the famous Greek poetess Sappho. Charaxus worshiped Rhodope and showered her with wealth, but it wasn't enough to keep her.

Rhodope discovered that other men would also give her precious jewels and other treasures in return for her affection, and she took them up on their offers as often as not. (Just what she did to express her affection is not clear from extant ancient history books.)

One day Rhodope was bathing in a river when an eagle flew off with one of her sandals. The bird carried its prize directly to King Psamtik of Egypt, who was outside his palace surrounded by his subjects. The king was astonished by the perfect proportions and small size of the sandal. He immediately demanded that its owner be brought to him. His soldiers found Rhodope in due time and brought her to the king. He apparently was unfazed by her history with other men and immediately asked her to become his queen. *His* treasures were substantial enough to win her heart, and she accepted. Shortly after their wedding, Rhodope commanded that work begin on a monument to herself, which would survive as long as her life story: Egypt's Third Pyramid of Gizeh.

Cinderella No. 2: Wife of the French Actor Thevenard (1700)

This young Cinderella lived with her parents in Paris. She was exceptionally pretty but very poor. The family had no money for new clothing or shoes, but they tried to keep their possessions in repair. Cinderella's slippers were being mended at the cobbler's shop one day when the famous French actor Thevenard passed by. He noticed the slipper and was enchanted by its smallness. He couldn't get it out of his mind and came back day after day to gaze at it. Finally, he asked the cobbler for the name of the shoe's owner, but the cobbler either could not or would not reveal her identity.

Thevenard was sixty-three years old and unmarried. As the days went by, he became obsessed with the unknown girl. He was determined to catch a glimpse of her, so he settled in across from the cobbler's stall to wait until she fetched her shoe. Eventually she appeared. Thevenard introduced himself and was charmed by her. Soon, despite his age and her poverty, the two were married.

Cinderella No. 3: Jakob and Wilhelm Grimm's Version (1800)

Cinderella No. 3 belongs to the Grimm's fairy tale version of the Cinderella story. Like today's Cinderella, she has a rich father, a hard-hearted stepmother, and two fat, ugly stepsisters, who force Cinderella to do all the chores around the house.

Cinderella was not her original name but a nickname. She had to sleep by the fireplace, where her clothes were often covered with soot and cinders, so her stepsisters dubbed her Cinderella.

One day her father was setting off for a fair several towns away, and he asked the three girls what he should bring each of them. The stepsisters demanded fine clothes and jewels, but Cinderella only asked for a sprig from the first branch to brush against him on his way home.

Cinderella's father brought back everything the girls had requested, including the sprig. Cinderella took it and planted it by her mother's grave. Whenever she visited the grave, she cried so much that her tears watered the sprig and it grew into a large tree. A little bird nested in the tree and became her friend.

Some months later, the king announced that there would be a grand three-day feast during which his son would select a bride. On the first day, Cinderella helped her stepsisters fix their hair and arrange their beautiful clothes, and when she was finished she begged her stepmother to allow her to go to the feast with them. The stepmother laughed at her, ridiculed her torn and dirty clothes, and finally flung a plate of peas into the fireplace, saying, "If you can pick out all these peas in two hours, then you can go to the feast." Cinderella quickly rallied her little bird friend. He brought hundreds of doves, and within one hour all of the peas had been retrieved.

This was not good enough, however. Cinderella's stepmother next threw two dishes of peas into the ashes and gave Cinderella one hour to pick them all out. Again the birds came, and in half an hour the work was done.

The stepmother still refused. Cinderella had no good clothes, she insisted. The girl couldn't dance, and she'd put the family to shame. With that, she and her daughters went off to the feast.

Feeling miserable, Cinderella went to sit beneath her tree. The little bird brought her a dress of gold and silver and spangled silk slippers for her feet. She put them on and quickly went after the others to the feast.

Cinderella was so transformed that her stepsisters didn't recognize her. They, as well as the prince, were enchanted by her beauty. The prince danced only with her all evening, and when the first evening ended, he insisted on seeing her home. She refused, and slipped away from him. He followed, but she hid in the pigeon house.

The prince waited until Cinderella's father came home, then asked for permission to look into the pigeon house to find the mystery beauty. They opened the coop, but Cinderella had fled through the back. She'd returned the beautiful clothes to the bird and dressed herself again in her rags.

The next night went just as the first. Cinderella arrived in splendor at the feast and danced with the prince all evening. He again saw her home, but this time she escaped into the branches of a large pear tree in her father's yard. With her father's consent, they chopped down the tree, but no one was there. Cinderella had managed to climb down the back of the tree and had changed into her old clothes.

On the third evening the bird brought her an even more beautiful dress and slippers of pure gold. When the feast ended, she ran from the prince in such a hurry that one of her slippers fell off. The prince took the shoe to her father and promised to marry the girl whose foot fit the shoe.

The eldest stepsister tried to put her foot into the slipper, but her big toe was much too large. Her mother proceeded to cut off the toe, and the shoe fit. As the prince was driving off with his bride-to-be, the little bird sang a song warning the prince to check the shoe. When the prince noticed the trickle of blood coming from the girl's foot, he promptly returned her and demanded that the next sister try the shoe.

The second sister got her foot almost all the way into the shoe, but her heel was too large. Her mother forced it in, but her heel began to bleed. The bird again warned the prince just in time, and so it was Cinderella's turn. When he saw that her foot fit the slipper perfectly, the prince finally recognized his dancing partner. This time as the two drove past, the bird sang a song of congratulations to the bride-to-be.

Cinderella No. 4: The Cinderella We Know Today

The modern-day Cinderella was created by French storytellers in the nineteenth century. She's a twin sister to the Cinderella of the brothers Grimm, but instead of a bird in a magical tree, this Cinderella has a fairy godmother.

This Cinderella also has two cruel stepsisters. But when *her* king announces the court ball, it's her fairy godmother who makes sure that Cinderella attends. With a whisk of her wand, this all-powerful fairy conjures a coach out of a pumpkin, zaps mice into horses, lizards into footmen, and frees trapped rats by transforming them into coachmen. For Cinderella's costume the godmother produces finery of gold, silver, and precious jewels. For her feet, the now-famous glass slippers. (It is possible that the slippers once upon a time in the French version were fur, one translation for which is *vair*. Fur would have been more practical—and valuable—than glass for use in a shoe. But *vair* sounds almost exactly like *verre*, the French word for "glass." Our current image of the slippers may be the result of a mistaken translation.)

Cinderella's fairy godmother gives the girl her gifts on the condition that she be home by midnight. If she's not on time, everything returns to its true state. Cinderella, of course, agrees, and hurries off to the ball, where she naturally wins the prince over with her beauty and charm. True to her word, she gets home just before the stroke of twelve. As a reward, her godmother agrees to provide the necessary accessories again the next night so she can return to the palace for a second ball.

The second night, however, Cinderella loses track of the time. The striking of the clock alerts her, and she barely gets out of the palace before the spell wears off. The only remnant of splendor are the glass slippers, one of which slips off her foot as she flees. For some unknown—but extremely convenient—reason, the slippers are exempt on this night (though not, apparently the first) from the magic's limitations.

Predictably, the prince searches every house in the country in order to find the owner of the glass slipper. When his pages arrive at Cinderella's house, her identity is revealed. The fairy godmother restores her fancy clothing. The good-hearted Cinderella forgives her rude stepsisters for all their past cruelty and marries the king's son. Of course, they live happily ever after.

Shoe Myths and Fables

Footwear plays a pivotal role in several myths and fables dating back to ancient times. Some of these stories are clearly fictional, but others tread the line between fact and fantasy. . . .

Boötes, the Herdsman

A northern constellation seen near the curve of Ursa Major's tail in the summer sky, Boötes is also a mythological figure. According to legend, Boötes was robbed of all his possessions by his own brother. After wandering the earth, he invented the plow. His mother, Callisto, was so impressed that she persuaded Zeus to place Boötes in the sky.

Orion, the Hunter

The son of Poseidon and Euryale, Orion was both powerful and boastful. When he announced that he could conquer any animal on earth, however, the god Apollo had had enough. He prompted a giant scorpion to sting Orion in the foot, killing him. To protect him from any further harm, the gods placed Orion in the heavens directly opposite but out of reach of Scorpio.

Achilles

When Achilles was an infant, his mother, the immortal sea nymph Thetis, held him by the heel and dipped him in a magic river to seal him from harm. Despite this ingenious attempt to protect him, Achilles ultimately died at the hands of Paris and Apollo, who shot an arrow into his heel, the one spot on his body that had not been bathed in the protective water.

Boot Hill

Located in Dodge City, Kansas, is Boot Hill, a burial ground for desperadoes of the Old West, which got its name from the old saying that those in black hats die with their boots on. The landmark acquired such fame that towns throughout the Old West created Boot Hills of their own.

Dracula's Shoes

Bela Lugosi, the actor whose name became synonymous with the character Dracula, became addicted in his later years to the merchandise of a Hollywood shoe store. In fact, the store was a front for a drug operation. When Lugosi died, the hearse carrying his body detoured up Santa Monica Boulevard to pass the store. The hearse driver insists he did not steer the car in this direction.

Great Shoe Lists

Footwear Foods, Flowers, etc.

FAVORITE SHOE FOODS

Boot leg whiskey
Cheese *wedges*
Filet of *sole*
Toast and *jellies*
Lace cookies
Licorice *laces*
Heels of bread
Mu *shu* pork
Pigs' *feet*
*Pumpe*rnickel bread
*Pump*kin pie
Shoestring potatoes
Singapore *sling* cocktail
Tongue sandwich
Tootsie Roll
*Gato*rade

SHOE FLOWERS

COMMON NAME	LATIN NAME (Genus or Species)	DESCRIPTION
Calceolaria	*Calceolaria*	Latin genus, name translates as "a little shoe"

COMMON NAME	LATIN NAME (Genus or Species)	DESCRIPTION
Gillyflower	*Dianthus caryophyllus*	Elizabethan name for the carnation, or clove pink
Yellow lady's slipper	*Cypripedium calceolus*	Wild orchid found in moist woods; named in the Latin for Cypris, or Venus, the goddess of love
Moccasin flower	*Cypripedium acaule*	Pink orchid resembling a moccasin
Pumpkin	*Cucurbita pepo*	Large, round, gourdlike fruit that grows on a vine
Rubber plant	*Ficus elastica*	Plant with large, glossy, leathery leaves
Sandalwort	*Thesium linophyllum*	British wildflower
Sandalwood	*Santalum*	Any one of several Indo-Malayan evergreen trees, such as white or red sandalwood, which have heavy, dark fragrant wood
Slipper flower	*Pedilanthus tithymaloides*	Tropical American flower
Slippery elm	*Ulmus rubra*	Wide-spreading hardwood tree with fragrant bark, used as a demulcent
Shoeflower (or Chinese hibiscus)	*Hibiscus rosa-sinensis*	Chinese flower with dark juice, which Chinese ladies used to blacken their shoes and eyebrows

SHOE ANIMALS

ANIMAL	LOCATION	DESCRIPTION
Mule	Worldwide	Offspring of a donkey and a horse
Mule deer	Western United States	Long-eared deer
Puma	North and South America	Resembles a jaguar but lacks the spots; also called mountain lion or cougar
Shoebill	White Nile, Africa	Member of the heron family; large wading bird with long legs and heavy, shoelike bill
Heeler	South American countries	Fighting cock that uses its heels
Water moccasin	Southeastern United States	Poisonous snake
Dogs	United States	Domesticated animals related to the fox, wolf, and jackal

2

THE HISTORICAL SHOE

In the centuries since the first prehistoric footwear was fashioned from grasses and hides, shoes have left their mark on cultures throughout the world. Feet and shoes have always been favorite targets of the superstitious, and footwear fads repeatedly have spawned catchphrases that turned into common sayings. From time to time a cobbler has earned his place in the history books for achievements outside of shoemaking. Occasionally shoes have even played a role in historically noteworthy crimes. In this section we'll take a look at the highlights of footwear's "walk through history," beginning with some recent news.

Shoe News Trivia

The Crimes of Feet

St. Louis, 1980
Mistaken identity was the apparent motive for the shooting death of the wife of a Levi's for Feet salesman at a hotel near Lambert Airport. The couple was in town to attend a regional sales meeting. Their hotel was a gathering spot for a ring of

local prostitutes, one of whom closely resembled the salesman's wife. According to police, this prostitute had a dispute
with her pimp, who in turn had hired a killer to shoot her. The
gunman instead shot the Levi's salesman's wife as she was
leaving the hotel to visit her parents. The pimp was prosecuted,
but was acquitted for lack of evidence.

Los Angeles, 1983

Status shoes became the motive for murder in a Los Angeles
inner-city neighborhood when a twenty-one-year-old former
gang member wearing Stacy Baldwin shoes was killed by three
rival gang members. At the time of his murder, Fernando Cercerer was wearing brand-new $100 patent leather lace-ups
known as Stacy Adams. According to police gang specialists,
the shoes are considered a status symbol among inner-city
teens. The assailants attacked Cercerer with a cane and a knife,
stripped him of his shoes and money, and strutted off for a
dinner of beer and chicken at a nearby all-night restaurant
before heading for home. Detectives speculated that it was the
dead man's footwear that had "done him in."

Los Angeles, 1984

A shoe man with the unlikely name of Angel was caught in the
parking lot of a shopping mall with about 95 pounds of mari-
juana and nearly 5 pounds of cocaine. Angel owned a string of
high-quality women's shoe stores in the Los Angeles area. He
had been watched by federal agents for some time before the
bust and reportedly had solicited a government informant to
kill a drug dealer in Buffalo, New York. He was arrested while
on his way into his shoe store, but not before he'd shot and
wounded the arresting agent.

Sparta, Wisconsin, 1984

Murder struck the sales force of the Freeman Shoe Company
on September 21, when the salesman Ron Lampe was gunned
down in the woods of western Wisconsin. Lampe was last seen
alive at Beiers Shoe Store in Winona, Minnesota. He was heading home from a regional shoe trade show in Minneapolis and
apparently had stopped at a rest area on a Wisconsin highway.

His abandoned car and suitcase were found in the rest-area parking lot. His shoe sample case was found some 40 miles down the highway. Lampe's body turned up in the Sparta Township woods twenty days after his disappearance. Suspects in the case are a twenty-five-year-old white male with dark hair and a cross earring in his left ear and a white blond female wearing heavy-rimmed glasses. After Lampe's death, the suspects charged more than $500 to Lampe's credit cards at local gas stations and K Marts. The story echoes an incident several years earlier in which a female sales manager for Levi's for Feet was killed while traveling in the Carolinas.

La Canada, California, 1984

"Rumors of my death have been greatly exaggerated." This statement certainly would have worked for the shoe retailer William C. Bailey after the local obituary columns reported him a goner. The La Canada Valley Sun bowed and scraped its way out of the snafu that confused Bill Bailey's Shoe Store owner with the recently deceased owner of Bill Bailey Radio and Television Service. It wasn't all bad though. Bill Bailey had the chance to sneak-preview his obituary well before his time.

San Diego, 1984

Tennis shoes were key evidence in the murder trial of the escaped convict Kevin Cooper. At issue: Did the sneakers that left bloody prints at the crime scene belong to the man accused of hacking four people to death in June 1983? Prosecutors and prison officials said yes. They claimed that the defendant had been issued the special shoes because of a foot problem while still in prison at the Chino Institution for Men. A witness claimed that the shoes appeared to be tan or brown leather, however. It would take more than tennis shoes to decide this case.

New York, 1984

When criminals hotfoot it away from their crimes, they leave behind some highly incriminating evidence—their footprints. According to the FBI, footprints can be as valuable as fingerprints in identifying suspects. By comparing size, manufacturer's sole patterns, wear patterns, and sole shape with the shoes of a suspect, investigators may be able to prove their case. Injection-molded soles are particularly helpful to detectives because they usually have air bubbles, created in the manufacturing process, that are unique to that shoe. Depending on the make and style of a given shoe, forensic experts may be able to pinpoint a suspect's occupation, life-style, or area of residence. They lift the footprints not just from the floor or earth, but also from kicked-in doors or any surface touched by the foot. In one case, an imprint was taken from the bald head of a victim. Frequently, the impression, in oil or water, is invisible to the naked eye, but with the help of modern forensic techniques it can still be useful in court. Over the years, forensic experts have kept track of the types of shoes worn by criminals. According to the FBI agent William Bodziak, there's one shoe that's a particular favorite among murderers: Converse basketball high-tops.

Shoe Signs, Spells, Chants, and Sayings
Verbal Footprints Across History

Los Angeles, 1985
When searching for the man behind the "Night Stalker" serial murders, investigators noticed that the killer wore a distinctive tennis shoe. Footprints collected at some murder scenes revealed a size 10 pair of Reebok high-top sneakers.

When Richard Ramirez, age twenty-five, was arrested for the crimes, another man breathed a sigh of relief. Carlton Bell, who resembled the killer, also wore the Reeboks . . . in a size 11.

Over the centuries, shoes have been endowed with a variety of magical powers by the superstitious. If you performed the proper ritual with them, your shoes could secure your marriage, cure your aches and pains, or predict your fortune. Some of the most popular shoe superstitions were recorded in ditties that remain to this day. Others have made their way into folklore throughout the world.

Favorite Shoe Spells

If you long to catch a glimpse of the man you'll marry, perhaps these rituals will help.

Point your shoes toward the street,
Leave your garters on your feet, put your stockings on your
head,
And you'll dream of the man you're going to wed.

For independent newlyweds, this Olde English practice is a
must for the wedding day.

When Britons bold
Wedded of old,
Sandals were backwards thrown
The pair to tell
That, ill or well,
The act was all their own.

If you find a hairpin, stick it in your shoe;
The next boy you walk with
Will be sure to marry you.

Before going to bed, sprinkle a sprig of rosemary and a sprig
of thyme three times with water. Place one in each shoe, and
put a shoe on either side of your bed. Then say,

St. Valentine that's to lovers kind,
Come ease the trouble of my mind,
And send the man that loves me true
To take the sprigs out of my shoe.

When you marry, remember that the bride should wear

Something old, something new,
Something borrowed, something blue,
and a penny in her shoe.
Something new, something old,
Something borrowed, something stoled.

Can you interpret the meaning of the wearing of your shoes?

Wear at the toe, spend as you go,
Wear at the side, be a rich bride,
Wear at the heel, spend a good deal,
Wear on the ball, live to spend all.

When you find a clover, do you know what to do with it?

Find a two, put it in your shoe;
Find a three, let it be;
Find a four, put it over the door;
Find a five, let it thrive.

One leaf for fame, one leaf for wealth,
One leaf for a faithful lover,
And one leaf to bring glorious health,
Are all in a four-leaf clover.

On what day are you "cut out" to buy a new pair of shoes?

Cut your nails Monday, cut them for health;
Cut them on Tuesday, cut them for wealth;
Cut them on Wednesday, you'll get some news;
Cut them on Thursday, a new pair of shoes;
Cut them on Friday, cut them for sorrow;
Cut them on Saturday, see your sweetheart tomorrow;
Cut them on Sunday, cut them for evil
And be all week as cross as the devil.

Shoe Words

Boot Camp

In medieval England the servants who cleaned the guests' boots were themselves called boots. The term came to refer to the youngest or newest recruits in clubs and organizations, and ultimately it was adopted by both British and American armed forces to describe training camps.

Bootlegger

The term became popular during Prohibition, when bootleggers illegally produced and sold liquor. It actually originated more than a century earlier. Pirates, as well as early members of the American merchant navy, wore high boots with broad tops, in which they often bootlegged—or smuggled—valuables.

Buck
Early Americans traded deerskins called bucks with the Indians. The skins were worth between 50 cents and $1. Over time, Americans adopted the word "buck" as slang for the dollar.

Clomp
The Dutch wooden shoe is called a *klomp*. It makes such a loud, heavy sound that the name was adopted into a verb meaning "to walk noisily."

Cop
American policemen used to wear copper tips on their boots as protection and to add punch to their kicks during scuffles. The copper left its mark in the form of a nickname.

Flapper
Freewheeling women in the Roaring Twenties liked to wear their galoshes unbuckled so that they would flap going down the street. The women became known as flappers.

Gams
Women of European and American high society in the sixteenth century wore a high, slim boot with a lot of names—gamashes, gamashoes, gambages, gambadoes, and gambes. All the names were boiled down to the slang term that today refers to women's legs.

Gumshoe
Policemen on walking beats used to wear shoes with gum rubber soles to soften the wear on their feet. The nickname carried over to detectives and stuck.

Heel
The part of the shoe that's dirtiest and most low-down also describes a great many unpleasant people.

Hotfoot It
The English poet Chaucer used the term "foot hot" to indicate great speed or swiftness. This has evolved into the verb "hot-foot," slang for "skedaddle."

Sabotage
Sabots were wooden cloglike shoes worn by European peasants in the Middle Ages. When the peasants rose up against their landlords, they trampled the crops with their sabots. Textile workers in France and Belgium showed their resentment of the Industrial Age by tossing their sabots into the machines that were stealing their jobs. The sabots came to represent the premeditated ruination of property, or sabotage.

Spat
In the nineteenth century leggings were worn over shoes to protect them from mud. The cloths were called spatterdashes. Because so much dirt flies back and forth during quarrels between lovers and friends, the disputes were described as spats.

Stogie
American slaveowners used to order boots for their slaves by measuring the feet against sticks and then sending the sticks to the manufacturer. The sticks, called stogas, bore a resemblance to the cigars that we now call stogies.

Upstart
Very early in the sixteenth century, the gentry took to wearing leggings that they called start-ups. As happened with most fashions at the time, the lower classes soon adopted these leggings in imitation of the well-to-do. Also in keeping with the patterns of the day, the gentry dropped the fashion as soon as the "upstarts" began wearing them, but the term "upstart" took hold as a description for impertinent social climbers, and it's still used today.

Well-Heeled
In seventeenth-century Europe high heels were a status symbol reserved by law for the nobility. In a manner of speaking, heels continue to characterize the wealthy today.

FOOTWEAR SAYINGS

Lace into
Lay by the heels
On a shoestring
Shoestring budget
One foot in the grave
Walk a mile in his shoes
Follow in his footsteps
He's back on his feet
I have two left feet
Don't tread on me
Fast on his feet
Step right up
Fleet-footed
Pussyfooting
Have cold feet
Give him a lacing
Put your foot down
Jump in with both feet
Stand on your own two feet
Getting off on the right foot
Put your foot in your mouth
Everyone on an equal footing
Can you fill his boots?
Thinking on your feet
Kick up your heels
Getting a toehold
Dancing on air
Toe the line
Boot it

Shoe dogs
Heel and toe
Out at the heels
Take to your heels
Barefoot and pregnant
If the shoe fits, wear it
The shoes make the man
Getting your feet wet
Down at the heels
Give him the boot
Cool your heels
Foot the bill
Stepping out
Lick my boots
Head over heels
Light on your feet
You can bet your boots
Get your foot in the door
The shoe is on the other foot
Put your best foot forward
I'm glad I'm not in his shoes
To die with your boots on
Where the shoe pinches
Doing the two-step
Take it step by step
Fancy footwork
Skip to my loo
Footnote
Skip out

Historical Footlines
Footwear Fashions Through the Ages

When mankind was young clothing served a purely protective function. Ever since that time, apparel has been evolving, with decorative form more often obscuring function than enhancing it. Shoes are no exception, as this "footline" illustrates.

CHRONOLOGY

TIME	PLACE	FASHION
Post–Ice Age	Worldwide	Although there are no surviving samples, archaeologists suspect that prehistoric humans wore footwear made of hides and grasses. In the warmer climates, they wove sandals. In colder regions, they fashioned fur-lined boots.
3500 B.C.– 1325 B.C.	Egypt	The first visual records of footwear are paintings found on tomb walls, showing sandals woven from papyrus. A tomb painting in Thebes dating from about 1470–1445 B.C. depicts a geometrically patterned sock-sandal resembling later Balkan and native American soled socks.
		Tutankhamun's tomb (c. 1325 B.C.) contained a pair of bejeweled sandals of dyed leather detailed with duck heads and lotus flowers. In ancient Egypt the more exotic the footwear, the higher the rank of the wearer.

TIME	PLACE	FASHION
		Sandals in ancient Egypt often had human images pressed into the soles. The images represented the wearer's enemy, the purpose being to symbolically crush the enemy with every step. Later, the Hebrews flipped the meaning and etched images of the wearer's beloved into the heel so that he might leave a mark of his love wherever he walked.
1500 B.C.	Assyria	Assyrians wore soft leather boots similar to native American buckskins. The boots had turned-up, moon-shaped toes similar to those still found in Turkish slippers, some Arab footwear, and Dutch clogs.
300 B.C.	Greece	The original platform shoes, called *korthonos,* were worn by Greek actors. The soles were made of solid cork, 3 to 4 inches thick, which made the actors seem larger than life and powerful as gods. Inside the soles the actors often inserted noisemaking devices so that each step would produce sounds, such as wheezing or clicking.
		Footwear evolved from sandals into shoes. The Greeks added *lingula,* which we now know as tongues—the leather strip that runs beneath the laces from the toes to the ankle. A patch of

TIME	PLACE	FASHION
		leather was added to protect the heel and ultimately became the heel of the shoe as we know it today.
55 B.C.–A.D. 41	Rome	The Romans created a soft leather boot that slipped into the sandal for outside wear but was worn as the only footwear when inside. Called *soccus,* it was the forerunner of the sock we wear today. It was also basically the same as the Japanese *tabi,* the cotton slipper-socks that are worn with platform *geta.* The original shoe sole was actually a shoe in itself—the *solea.* This thin slip of leather, strapped loosely to the foot, was worn indoors. Children, peasants, philosophers, and priests wore *baxea,* a sandal made of fiber. Roman soldiers wore *caligae,* gladiator sandals with spiked soles. Gaius Caesar Germanicus (A.D. 12–41) was nicknamed Caligula (Little Boot) because he was raised around army camps and because he himself wore *caliga.*
A.D. 900	China	The Chinese tradition of binding women's feet originated with the fashions of palace dancers but spread to all women in China except nuns, slaves, and some prostitutes. The bound foot was referred to as a lotus foot and was

TIME	PLACE	FASHION
		thought to enhance a woman's sexual powers. Men who married a woman with bound feet sometimes took a second wife without bound feet to serve as a slave to wife number one. The fetish for tiny feet in women took hold and intensified over the following centuries until 1911, when the Republic finally put a stop to the custom.
1066	England	The Norman conquerors brought simple but occasionally whimsical footwear to the British Isles. The favorites were low boots and shoes with pointed or turned-up toes. Some of the toes were shaped like fishtails or stretched and twisted into the shape of a ram's horn. The shaped toes were stuffed with moss, hay, or wool to keep them firm.
		Under the Normans, shoemakers split into three guilds—tanners, cobblers, and cordwainers. Cordwainers were top-of-the-line bootmakers who owed their title to Córdoba, Spain, home of the prized horsehide called cordovan leather.
1300	England	After the Crusades, the British and French succumbed to a superstitious claim that pointy-toed shoes were protection against witches. Fashion obligingly extended the toes to

TIME	PLACE	FASHION

as long as a foot or more. In England the shoes were called crakows, and in France, *poulaines*. The length of the toe became an indication of status: the longer the toe, the more difficult it was to walk and therefore the more leisurely— and presumably wealthy—the life-style of the wearer. Shoes with toes longer than the length of the foot were held up by means of a chain, which connected the toe to a band around the knee.

Europeans in this era also wore pattens, slip-on platforms worn over shoes to protect them from mud and bad weather. Pattens were made of metal or wood and were worn into the nineteenth century.

1320 — England King Edward II established sizing for shoes. Three barleycorns equaled 1 inch. The longest available foot measured 39 barleycorns, or 13 inches, so the largest shoe was called size 13. Smaller sizes were marked off by decreases of 1 barleycorn, or a third of an inch. The same basic system is used today. Including the various widths, there are more than 300 different sizes all together.

TIME	PLACE	FASHION
1500	England	The duck bill look was an extreme reaction to the crakow. Instead of having long pointed toes, the duckbills were wide and squat in the toe. The height of fashion was a leather bar shoe lined with brightly colored satin and strategically slashed so that the satin puffed through the leather. Instead of stretching lengthwise, the duckbills stretched in width. Just as the leisure class formerly wore long crakows, now they wore the widest duckbills they could find. Queen Mary (1516–1558) ultimately ruled that 6 inches was the limit and the trend-setters backed down.
1550	England	The Elizabethans coined the word "slipper" for footwear worn only indoors. Their shoes were still lined like the duckbills, but they were sleek, and only glimpses of lining showed. When traveling, Elizabethans attached special hollow heels to their shoes and hid jewelry inside the heels to avoid robbery by highwaymen.
1550	France	Italy's Catherine de Médicis (1519–1589) brought the high heel and the ballet shoe to France when she married Henry II. The ballet shoes were worn by male and female court entertainers. They had heels, which did not

TIME	PLACE	FASHION
		vanish until the eighteenth century, when the French dancer Marie-Anne de Camargo insisted that the heel be removed from her ballet slippers.
1600	America	Native American Indians originated the shoe we now call the moccasin. It's unclear exactly when the style developed, but it has evolved into a broad range of styles reflecting the different aesthetics and resources of various tribes. Traditional Indian moccasins incorporated intricate patterns of beadwork, quills, embroidery, and other design work.
1600	Italy	Chopines were the ultimate platform shoes for women, and they were a big hit in Venice. The fashion of ornamental shoes on stiltlike pedestal soles came originally from Turkish harems and later spread to England before dying out around the end of the seventeenth century. The soles were anywhere from 2 inches to a foot or more in height and were often elaborately carved or detailed. The pedestals took a variety of shapes. Some were shaped like an hourglass, with the center of the foot resting on the main support. Others were cut out deeply at the front or back to give the foot a look of

TIME	PLACE	FASHION

flying. The English diarist John Evelyn, who in 1645 visited Venice, wrote the following description of women wearing chopines: "Thus attired, they set their hands on the heads of two matron-like servants, or old women, to support them . . . it is ridiculous to see how these ladies crawl in and out of their gondolas, by reason of their chopines and what dwarfs they appear, when taken down from their wooden scaffolds." The shoes were also given mention in Shakespeare's *Hamlet:* "By'r Lady, your ladyship is nearer to heaven than when I saw you last, by the altitude of a chopine." Chopines eventually were banned by the Venetians for fear that a pregnant woman might fall while wearing them and miscarry.

| 1650 | France | The reign of Louis XIV brought men's footwear fashion to new heights of exaggeration. The short King favored high heels, and ultimately heels as high as 5 inches came into vogue for aristocratic men. Boots were spurred and had broad cuffs that sailed out around the leg. The cuffs were richly lined with lace and ruffles. Some of the boots were worn with slip-on platform soles, which were attached at the toe and which shuffled like clogs |

TIME	PLACE	FASHION

when walking. Louis XIV was entitled to wear the most outrageous clothes in the country, and he did. One of his favorite styles was a red high-heeled shoe tied with bows that extended 8 inches on either side of the knot; each of the remaining lengths of red lacing were bowed, and in their centers were decorative rosettes.

1629   America   Thomas Beard and Isaac Rickman became the first shoemakers in America. Summoned by Governor William Bradford of Massachusetts to become his personal cobblers, they landed in Salem on the third voyage of the Mayflower. One year later Francis Ingalls arrived from Lincolnshire, England, to become the first tanner in America. He set up shop in Lynn, Massachusetts, which would eventually become a major center for shoe manufacturing in this country. The first full-fledged tannery was started in New York by the Eversteen Brothers.

1660   England   Samuel Pepys invented the buckle to replace the latchet, which had been worn for the previous 200 years. The latchet was a method of folding shoe tops and heel flaps and securing them with a leather thong. Pepys's buckles were the same

TIME	PLACE	FASHION
		ones worn by the Pilgrims when they arrived in America.
1700	France	Fashion had fun with shoes until the French Revolution did away with whimsy of any kind, in fashion and elsewhere. Shoemakers embroidered sayings or painted pictures on the heels of expensive shoes. Heels were shaped like hearts so that they'd leave impressions of romantic emblems on garden paths. Novelty heels were in style until 1789.
1750	America	A Welsh shoemaker named John Adams Dagyr opened the first shoe factory in Lynn, Massachusetts. The work was all done by hand, but the laborers worked on individual pieces of the final product in assembly-line fashion.
1790	France	Shoelaces were introduced. Called shoestrings, they were used in place of buckles. Thomas Jefferson was among the first to wear laces in America. He was denounced for caving in to the "foppish French fad."
1791	England	In England's buckle capital, Birmingham, 20,000 people were laid off by the town's buckle manufacturer as the fashion for buckles waned. The Prince of Wales was called in to provide assistance, but although he himself continued to wear

TIME	PLACE	FASHION
		buckles, the vogue could not be revived.
1794	America	The shoemaker brothers Quincy and Harvey Reed opened the first retail shoe store at 133 Broad Street in Boston.
1804	France	In Napoleon's day women wore soft slippers without heels. Empress Josephine reportedly complained that one of her slippers had developed a hole after just one wearing. Her shoemaker replied, "I see what it is. Madame, you have walked in them!" Men in the Napoleonic era were taken with the military look, and all their boots acquired tassels, colored leather insignia and linings.
1810	France	Patent leather first appeared in men's pumps and women's boots. This selective use of patent lasted for a century.
1811	America	Elisha Hobart invented shoe nails, which eventually replaced the wooden shoe pegs that had been used to fasten soles to uppers.
1816	Italy	The singer Luigi Marchesi reached the height of popularity in Milan, and women throughout the city wore his portrait as a clasp to each shoe.
1822	America	The first set of lasts for right and

TIME   **PLACE**   **FASHION**

left feet was produced in
Philadelphia. Up to this time
there was no difference between
a right and left shoe. The
innovation was ahead of its time,
however, and the footwear made
on these lasts were called
crooked shoes. Not until the Civil
War did the notion of right versus
left become widely accepted.

About this same time the
American cowboy created the
cowboy boot, a thick pull-on
boot with a narrow squared-off
toe and a high squared heel. The
toe slipped easily into a stirrup.
The heel prevented the toe from
slipping too far forward and
helped the cowboy brace himself
on the ground while roping
cattle.

Two-toned footwear began to
migrate from France to America,
as indicated by Thomas
Jefferson's brown boots with buff
tops. These were called co-
respondent's shoes. In due time,
women's shoes were both two-
toned and two-textured. By 1840
women were wearing boots
combining fabric uppers with
patent leather toes, linen uppers
with leather bottoms, and suede
with leather trim and soles.
Women in the Victorian era wore
only boots for outside; slippers
and low shoes were restricted to
inside wear.

TIME	PLACE	FASHION
1828	France	Flat pumps tied over the instep were introduced as men's footwear. At first, they were worn only by footmen, but after the French Revolution this simple style became everyone's favorite.
1839	America	Charles Goodyear accidentally discovered the process of vulcanizing rubber, which launched the rubber footwear industry and paved the way for sneakers and other athletic shoes. In 1842 the Candee Rubber Company of New Haven, Connecticut, introduced the first rubber footwear. Unfortunately, the shoes cracked in the winter and melted in the summer.
1840	Sweden	The buffing process used to make suede originated in Sweden. The French dubbed the leather Swede, which sounded like suede, and the name stuck. The first suede was produced in America in 1865.
1868	America	The first sneakers, with gum rubber soles, came into vogue for the upper classes. They were called croquet sandals. Similar shoes, but with leather uppers, were later popular among detectives and policemen, which is how they came to be known as gumshoes.
1889	America	The chic shoe for women was a high-top cloth boot with fourteen

TIME	PLACE	FASHION
		buttons. In 1893 slide fasteners, now called zippers, were invented for shoes—much to the relief of the shoe salesmen and women who'd spent four years buttoning and unbuttoning their high-tops.
1900	America	The trend away from boots toward shoes began with the introduction of gaiters. Made of felt, canvas, or leather, gaiters pulled around the leg and buttoned up the side from the ankle to the knee. They allowed people to wear shoes without losing the protective feeling of boots. By 1923 gaiters were replaced by colored stockings, and the switch to low shoes was complete.
1909	America	The first long-distance running shoe was manufactured by The Spalding Company. It was a leather high-top with rubber soles, each single pair weighed 2 pounds.
1911	China	With the founding of the Chinese Republic, footbinding was outlawed. Women were entitled to walk again.
1934	America	The first open-toed sandals appeared in Miami. The shoe style that formerly symbolized poverty suddenly became *de rigueur*. Since the thirties, the

TIME	PLACE	FASHION
		fashion world has felt free to switch styles from season to season. Although there are always current fads, the second half of the twentieth century basically has been an era of "anything goes."
1984	America	Puma invented the first "computer shoe." Designed to attach to a home computer after each run, this running shoe yields a printout describing the distance covered, the number of calories burned, and the quality of performance.

Shoemaking with the Colonists

Today's business executives may pride themselves on "dressing for success," but the prize for *packing* for success goes to the Massachusetts Bay Puritans. There were no shoemakers among the Puritans, and they didn't expect to find any in the wilderness of the New World, so the Puritans took no chances. On arrival in America in the early seventeenth century, each Puritan carried at least four pairs of quality footwear.

The Pilgrims who came to America on the *Mayflower* were another story. Landing in Plymouth after being exiled from Holland, these new arrivals had neither extra shoes nor equipment to make shoes. The shortage of footwear quickly assumed epidemic proportions, prompting Governor William Bradford to summon the shoemaker Thomas Beard to the Colonies on the third trip of the *Mayflower*. Beard and his apprentice, Isaac Rickman, arrived in 1629 with eight simple

THE TREE OF SHOE HISTORY
From Grass Sandals to Granny Boots

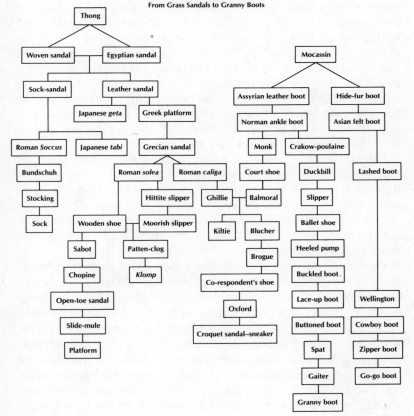

tools—a knife, awl, needle, pincers, lapstone, hammer, stirrups, and last. By 1760 the city of Philadelphia alone had more than 300 master shoemakers and twice that many journeymen and apprentices. Cobblers, shoe repair men, had by that time branched off into a separate profession.

Colonial shoemaking bore little resemblance to shoemaking today. Most shoemakers didn't have shops of their own. Instead, they carried their tools with them as they traveled across the country. At each farm they'd stop and stay for several days, long enough to make shoes for every member of the family with leather supplied by the customer. Since his tools lent themselves to a variety of essential tasks, the cobbler became a jack-of-all-trades. He used his pincers to pull teeth, his lapstone to sharpen blades, and his hammer and awl to perform an assortment of carpentry jobs. His travels also exposed him to the latest gossip for miles around, so he became a valued source of news and information.

Not until the eighteenth century did the "home stage" of colonial shoemaking give way to the "handicraft stage" and the development of independent shoemaker's shops, which turned out "bespoke work" for local customers. The village shoemaker was considered a craftsman, and the profession had become so attractive that apprentices worked for seven years to become full-fledged shoemakers.

The craft of shoemaking began making the transition to industry through the enterprise of John Adams Dagys, known in the trade as the Father of American shoemaking. Up until 1750, it was standard practice for one cobbler to execute an entire shoe, start to finish. Dagys introduced the notion of the assembly line by assigning one worker to cutting, one to lasting, one to boring holes, one to stitching, and so forth. The pace of production picked up so quickly that these early shoe factories for the first time began to turn out "unordered" or "sale shoes," which were not ordered ("bespoken") in advance. In 1794 in Boston, the shoemakers Quincy and Harvey Reed opened the first American retail store to sell these ready-made shoes, and by the mid-nineteenth century the invention of a wide range of shoemaking machinery transformed the art of shoemaking into a mechanized industry.

Shoemakers Who Made History
From Conquerors to Saints

Shoes are only part of the story of footwear history. As the following profiles demonstrate, shoemakers have contributed more than their share to making the time—or foot—lines interesting.

DATE	SHOEMAKER	ACCOMPLISHMENTS
c.1027–1087	William the Tanner aka William the Conqueror (illegitimate son of Robert, duke of Normandy, and Arlette, daughter of a tanner)	Conquered England in 1066, beginning the rule of the House of Normandy, which lasted until 1135
1244–1334	Pope John XXII (born in a shoemaker's shop in Cahors, France)	Served as pontiff from 1316 to 1334 (not including the illegitimate claim of Nicholas V to the papacy in 1328). After the death of Clement V, John convinced the Vatican conclave to let him select the next pope, then chose himself. He was known for his love of money and his willingness to bless divorces and unorthodox marriages, as long as the price was right. History books report

DATE	SHOEMAKER	ACCOMPLISHMENTS
		that by the time he died he'd stashed away somewhere between 1 and 5 million gold florins weighing more than 2 tons.
c. 1340–1400	Geoffrey Chaucer (the family interests were those of wine and leather trades)	English poet, author of *The Canterbury Tales*. Chaucer means maker of chausses, a kind of footwear, essentially the equivalent of shoemaker.
16th century	Gabriel Capellini	Italian shoemaker-painter
1574–1623	Francesco Brizzio	Italian shoemaker-painter
1616–?	Ludolph De Jong	Flemish shoemaker-painter
1624–1691	George Fox (apprenticed in youth to a shoemaker in Leicestershire, England)	Founder of the Society of Friends (Quakers)
c. 1636–1674	Thomas Traherne (son of a shoemaker)	British poet and prose writer, author *Centuries of Meditation*
17th century	Sir Thomas Tichborne	English cobbler who became lord mayor of London in 1656

DATE	SHOEMAKER	ACCOMPLISHMENTS
17th century	Nicholas Lestage	Created for Louis XIV of France the first recorded seamless boots. In recognition of this accomplishment, his portrait was hung in the royal gallery with this poem: "Great the fame of him portrayed/Was, and none and naught could dim it;/When his wondrous boot he made,/Mind and art had reached their limit."
1694–1774	John Smart (cobbler of Kettering, England)	"Most Prolific Shoemaker" (our designation); contributed his part to the production of thirty-four children by five wives
19th century	Joseph Staub (shoemaker to the court of the Bourbons, France)	Discovered in 1820 by Vicomtesse de Save, who called him king of shoemakers; Staub replied that he'd rather be "shoemaker to kings," and she took the hint
19th–20th centuries	Wilhelm Voigt (cobbler of Koepenick, Germany)	In 1906, masquerading as a captain in the Kaiser's army, Voigt

DATE   **SHOEMAKER**   **ACCOMPLISHMENTS**

took the mayor of
Koepenick prisoner
and requisitioned the
town treasury. After
sending his prisoner
under guard to Berlin,
Voigt was sentenced
to four years in
prison. The feat
attracted admirers,
who sent Voigt gifts
and after his release
set him up in London,
where he sold
autographed
postcards.

Dorothy, her ruby slippers, and her friends.
From the MGM release *The Wizard of Oz* © *1939 by Loew's Incorporated.*
Ren. 1966 Metro-Goldwyn-Mayer Inc.

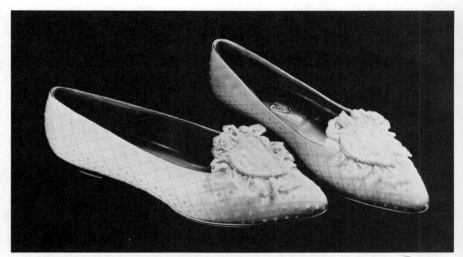

The wedding slippers of H.R.H. the Princess of Wales. Designed and handmade by Clive Shilton.
Courtesy of Clive Shilton. Photograph by Theo Bergstrom.

Clive Shilton making a personal appearance with his custom-made shoe-and-accessory collection at the Right Bank Shoe Company, a posh shoe boutique in Beverly Hills. He is accompanied by partner Julie Smith.
Photograph by Alan Berliner.
Courtesy of the Right Bank Shoe Company.

The stars come out for Fancy Footwear. Leslie Uggams, Mary Martin, and Carol Channing graced the opening of Wilkes Bashford's new women's clothing and footwear store in San Francisco in 1984.

Polly Bergen and samples from her own footwear line.
Courtesy of Poco Industries. Photograph by Starr Black.

A Pair of Boots (1887). Painted in
Paris by Vincent van Gogh.
The Shoe (1975–1977) by Richard
Lindner.
　　Courtesy Galerie Maeght
Lelong, New York.

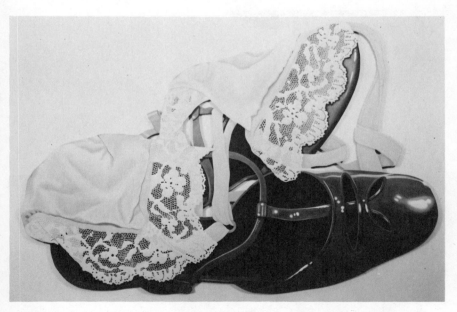

Pink Bra & Blue Shoes (1981) by Tom Wesselmann. Wesselmann's fascination
with footwear extended to two other works as well: *Still Life with Belt &
Sneaker* (1979–1981) and *Sneakers & Purple Panties* (1981).
　　Courtesy of Sidney Janis Gallery, New York.

The cast of *Ain't Misbehavin'* © Gacci.

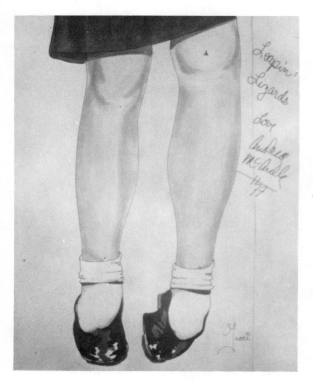

Andrea McArdle in *Annie*
© Gacci.

A Chorus Line © Gacci.

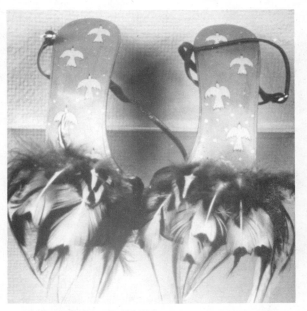

Closet. Mixed media installation by Cecilia Brunazzi, 1984.
Courtesy of Cecilia Brunazzi. © 1984 Simo Neri.

Another company with an innovative advertising campaign is Hang Ten International. Once the sole property of surfers, the trademark footprints now have taken to the road, the slopes, and even to the sky!

Funny looking

You've probably heard of them. Birkenstock sandals. Funny looking, sure, but only if you put fashion ahead of incredible comfort. Birkenstock sandals shape to your feet like cool, soft sand. They give you support and improve your posture and circulation to let you walk healthier, more naturally. And they last and last. Birkenstock. Made funny looking so you can smile more wearing them. 20 men's and women's styles from $27 to $74. You've gone without them long enough.

Birkenstock ®

(DEALER IMPRINT)

Reverse snobbery is the gimmick behind Birkenstock's eccentric advertising campaign. This footwear has gone beyond art and design to the bare essence of function. Its very ugliness becomes its selling point!
    Courtesy of Birkenstock.

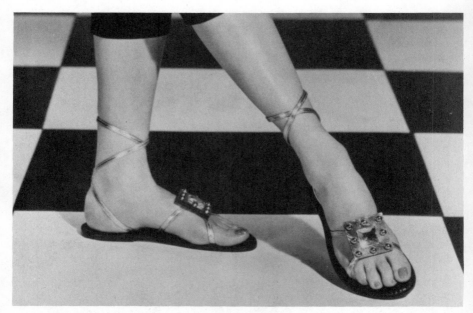

These bejeweled sandals by Bernardo are modeled on the footwear of ancient Egyptian rulers, whose footwear was studded with precious gems and metals.
Reprint of original photography. Courtesy of Bernardo, Columbus, Ohio.

The ancient Greeks created the tongue. Bernardo brought it back into sandals with this version, marketed in the 1950s.
Reprint of original photography. Courtesy of Bernardo, Columbus, Ohio.

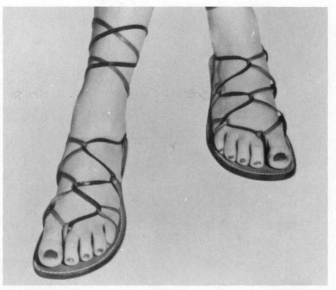

The essential Roman sandal was simply a sole, or *solea,* strapped to the foot or leg with long laces. In the 1950s Bernardo used the same design principle to create several different versions of the "strap" sandal.

Reprint of original photography. Courtesy of Bernardo, Columbus, Ohio.

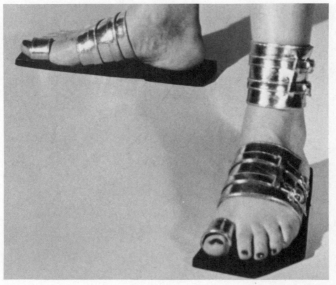

Bernardo first revived the Roman gladiator sandal in the 1960s and called it a Cuff sandal. With its metallic straps and angular design, the sandal was tough-looking even without the spikes that characterized the original Roman version.

Reprint of original photography. Courtesy of Bernardo, Columbus, Ohio.

THE ORIGINAL GHILLIE
Britain circa 100 B.C.

BAXEA: A CHILDREN'S
SANDAL
Roman 55 B.C. - A.D. 700

SOCCUS : THE ORIGINAL SOCK
ROMAN 55 B.C. - 700 A.D.
(made of leather or wool, worn with leather sandal)

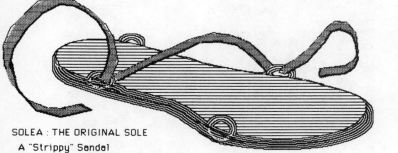

SOLEA : THE ORIGINAL SOLE
A "Strippy" Sandal
Rome 55 B.C. - A.D. 700

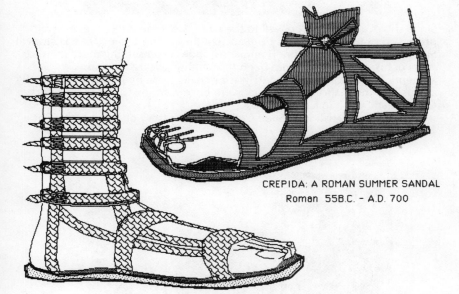

CREPIDA: A ROMAN SUMMER SANDAL
Roman 55B.C. - A.D. 700

THE ORIGINAL GLADIATOR SANDAL
Roman Britain 55 B.C. - A.D. 700

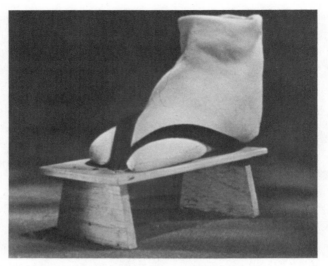

Since shoes don't stand up well to the ravages of time, there are few well-preserved examples of shoes from ancient times. The Thom McAn Historical Shoe Collection consists of 141 miniature shoes representing more than 4,000 years of history. Each style has been thoroughly researched and authenticated. This Japanese *geta* was orignally worn by Japanese monks. It's a cousin to the platform shoes that were once worn by Greek stage actors. *Geta* are still worn in Japan today.

Thom McAn Historical Shoe Collection. Courtesy of Thom McAn Shoe Company.

This Roman senator's shoe immediately characterized its wearer as a man of power and wealth. Notice the square-cut upturned toe and thick leather sole. The metal side fastening was in the shape of a "C" (Roman numeral for 100), standing for the one hundred members of the Senate.

Thom McAn Historical Shoe Collection. Courtesy of Thom McAn Shoe Company.

In tenth-century France the fashion setters considered this half-boot
Brodequin an essential element of their wardrobe.
Thom McAn Historical Shoe Collection. Courtesy of Thom McAn Shoe
Company.

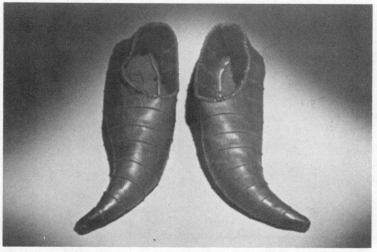

The flamboyant style of dress in fourteenth-century England was
characterized by sweeping curves and contorted forms. These "splay-foot"
shoes were typical of the times.
Thom McAn Historical Shoe Collection. Courtesy of Thom McAn Shoe
Company.

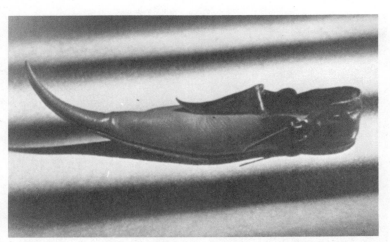

In fourteenth-century England this shoe was called a Crakow. In France it was the *Poulaine*. The longest version of this shoe was so cumbersome that the toe had to be held up by means of a chain attached to the waist.

Thom McAn Historical Shoe Collection. Courtesy of Thom McAn Shoe Company.

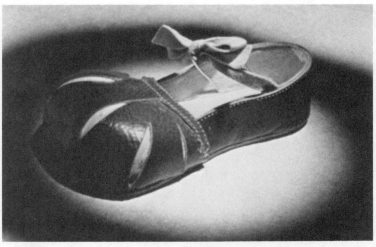

The trend toward broad toes went to extremes in northern Europe in the sixteenth century. These Duckbill shoes reached a width of ten inches and featured the same decorative slashes found on the sleeves and trousers of the clothing of the period.

Thom McAn Historical Shoe Collection. Courtesy of Thom McAn Shoe Company.

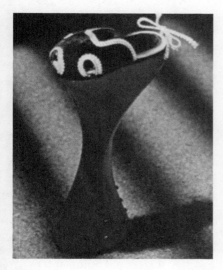

In seventeenth-century Venice, members of the leisure class wore chopines to make themselves appear taller. Those who wore the shoes had to be propped up on either side by servants in order to walk.

Thom McAn Historical Shoe Collection. Courtesy of Thom McAn Shoe Company.

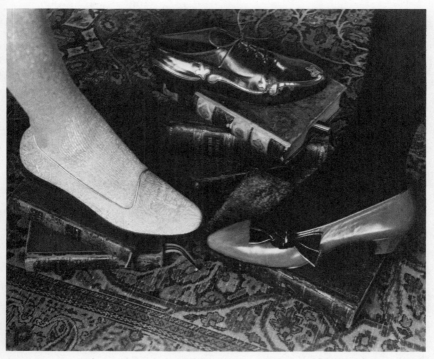

Renaissance shoes reborn. Elegant queen's slippers, heraldic tie-shoes, and courtly pumps make a comeback in twentieth-century versions.
Courtesy of the Footwear Council. © 1984 by James Dee Daley.

U.S. hand-turned child's shoe with a straight last. Made by Laird, Schober and Mitchell in 1876.
Courtesy of the Western Shoe Associates. Photograph by Alexandra Milovanovich.

Hand-turned high pearl-gray Grisson's kid boot. Made by the George E. Keith Company in 1914.
Courtesy of the Western Shoe Association. Photograph by Alexandra Milovanovich.

The spat, brogue, and Victorian bootie reappear in 1984 as historical shoe fashions come full circle.
Courtesy of the Footwear Council. © by James Dee Daley.

DRINK

Coca-Cola

DELICIOUS AND REFRESHING

A tour of footwear fashions since 1886. In the hundred years since its founding, the Coca-Cola Company has kept archives of virtually all its advertising. As we see in these pictures, the ads illustrate not only America's unchanging appetite for Coke but also its constantly shifting attitudes and fashions—including footwear fashions.

In the Roaring Twenties, American woman finally began to learn how to have fun. Baring flesh was part of the fun, but when they reached the beach, women still weren't ready to go *all* the way. Their shoes and even their socks stayed on.
    Courtesy of the Coca-Cola Company.

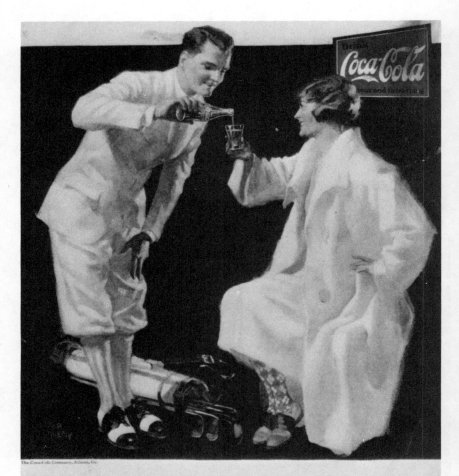

RECREATION AND REFRESHMENT
Go hand in hand ~ Wherever you
want refreshment, Coca-Cola fills
the need ~ Sold in 30 countries

Recreation and refreshment demanded just the right footwear in the stylish
twenties. Two-toned co-respondent's shoes and saddle oxfords hit the spot
for the country club set.

Courtesy of the Coca-Cola Company.

The footwear and swimwear fashion duet remained in vogue through the 1930s even among Hollywood starlets. Blond bombshell Jean Harlow posed scantily clad, but always kept her shoes on.
Courtesy of the Coca-Cola Company.

The carefree fashions of the 1920s and early 1930s turned to military issue with the onset of World War II. Women assumed both the role and look of serious national defenders. Sensible shoes were the name of the game.
Courtesy of the Coca-Cola Company.

Be really refreshed! Bowl with Coke! Only Coca-Cola gives you the cheerful lift that's bright and lively... the cold crisp taste that deeply satisfies! No wonder Coke refreshes you best!

The pause that most refreshed the American family of the 1950s was a trip to the local bowling alley. The bowling shoe industry has never been the same since.

Courtesy of the Coca-Cola Company.

What a **REFRESHING NEW FEELING**

...what a special zing...you get from Coke! The cold crisp taste and lively lift of Coca-Cola send you back shopping with zest. No wonder Coke refreshes you best!

With the arrival of the 1960s, comfort seemed a pleasure of the past. High heels, pointed toes . . . the look of the shoe took precedence over its fit, so that the only refreshing new feeling most women experienced was the feeling of no shoes at all.

Courtesy of the Coca-Cola Company.

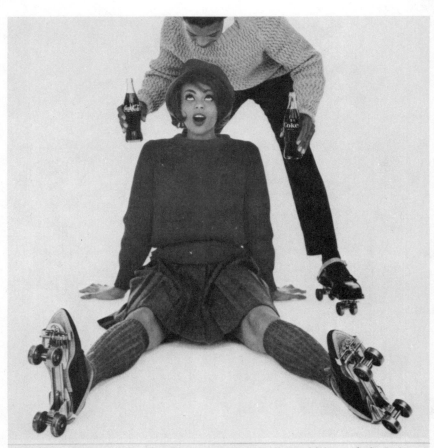

Things go smoother refreshed. Coca-Cola, never too sweet, gives that special zing... refreshes best.

things go
better
with
Coke

Drink *Coca-Cola*

Sometimes, even when the shoe fits, things could go better. This ad from the early 1970s reflects the beginning of the roller-skating craze in this country. By the time the fad peaked around 1980, skating had been transformed into a cross between dance and athletics. Roller-skate manufacturers felt the way bowling shoe manufacturers had felt in the 1950s.
    Courtesy of the Coca-Cola Company.

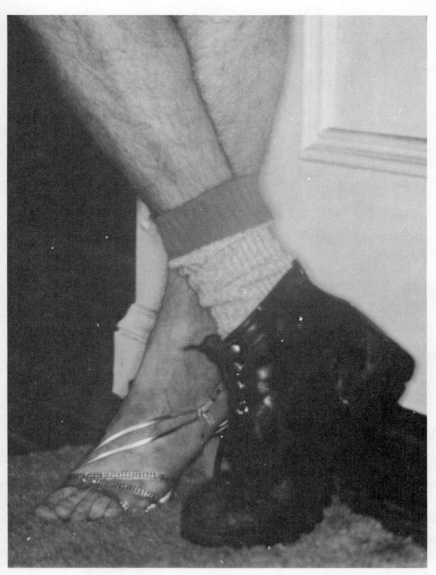

According to psychiatrists, most true shoe fetishists are men. Some go for "butch," some for glamour.

Courtesy of Bill Bernardo. From "The Butch Manual" © by Bill Bernardo.

A foot fetishist's dream. Today's "Cinderella slipper" lets it all show through. Courtesy of Stuart Weitzman.

"After Five" is a euphemism for sexy evening fashions. Worn with the mandatory dark sheer stockings, these four shoes incorporate the essential qualities of sexy footwear. From left: open toe, black silk, and rhinestones set off this high-heeled pump by DeLiso; black silk straps, open heel, and open toe mark the evening sandal by Nine; black satin, bugle beads, open back, and a high skinny heel spark up this sling by Stuart Weitzman for Martinique; black satin, silver kidskin, open toe, and stiletto heel make this Garolini sling a classic sexy shoe.

Courtesy of the Footwear Council. © by James Dee Daley.

Truly sexy fashions never really change. They invite and challenge at the same
time. They're dark and sultry but also flashy. From head to toe they signal
body heat.

Casadei. Courtesy of Electra Casadei.

CONSTRUCTION OF THE CHINESE TINY SHOE
NORTHERN STYLE FROM 1920'S

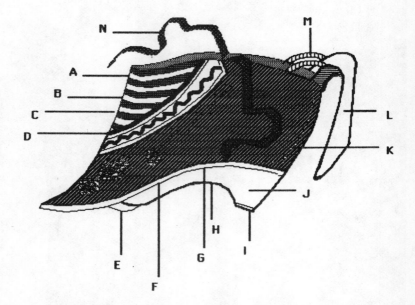

A. The "gate" of the shoe,
   called Moon or Temple Gate

B. "Ladder rungs" pull closed when worn

C. Bound foot surface

D. Point of the shoe's opening, or aperture

E. Front sole support

F. Border strip

G. Middle joint

H. Center of the Sole

I. Rear sole support

J. Perfume storage niche

K. Inner heel support

L. Heel lift

M. Heel lift reinforcement

N. Shoe fasteners

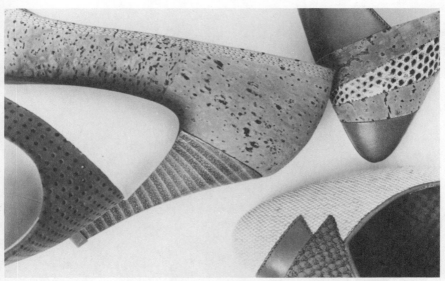

Color, texture, and pattern are all essential ingredients of shoe design. How they're mixed and matched can determine the essential "look" of a season. Courtesy of the Footwear Council. © 1984 by James Dee Daley.

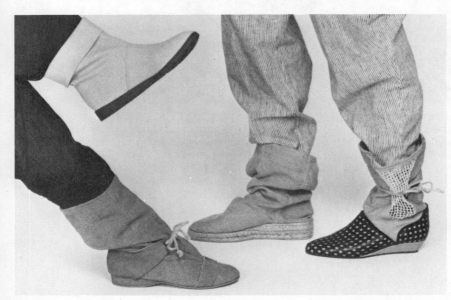

Boots gone athleisure, for summer 1984. Clockwise from lower left: linen boot with rope tie from Kenneth Cole; denim on poly bottom from Hang Ten; espadrille boot in crushed linen from Perry Ellis; linen and leather from Georgette Ghica.
Courtesy of the Footwear Council. © 1984 by James Dee Daley.

The exotics surface periodically as a popular style category. The term refers to the skins and patterns, which originate in the animal kingdom. From left: python stenciled pump by Stuart Weitzman for Mr. Seymour; zebra-look boot by La Marca; leopard ankle boot by Seven Star.

Courtesy of the Footwear Council. © 1984 by James Dee Daley.

3

SEX AND THE SINGLE SHOE

Down and Dirty

Will the Real Foot Fetishist
Please Stand Up

We all know people who have closets full of shoes, who *live* in shoe stores, and who simply *must* have matching shoes for every outfit. We may jokingly call these people shoe fetishists, but in fact, most of them are simply fashion mavens with a particular passion for footwear. True shoe and foot fetishists don't just look at or wear shoes—they *physically mate* with them.

Fetishists don't necessarily drool over the latest footwear fashions, nor do they always have large collections of shoes. Some don't even like shoes, but prefer feet in their natural state. True foot and shoe fetishists tend to be very particular about the objects of their desire—and about the ways they like their fetishes "served up."

According to the definition of fetishism that's most commonly used by psychiatrists, this sexual predilection can involve actual physical activity using the fetish (also spelled fetich), or it can rely primarily on fantasy. Freud viewed shoes as a "symbol of the female genitals." With this consciously or subconsciously in mind, some male fetishists rub or press the shoe against their genitals to achieve orgasm. Others simply stare at a shoe while fantasizing about its owner. The fetish may be a necessary aid to sexual activity, or, in what are described as pathological cases, it may replace the sexual partner entirely. Whatever the method, the ultimate objective is the same and the *fetish* is the object or situation that inspires sexual arousal. Psychological and psychiatric surveys indicate that shoe and foot fetishes are the most common forms of erotic symbolism, with foot fetishists outnumbering other types of fetishists by about 3 to 1. According to clinical reports, most shoe fetishists are men. Other fetishes include

- Any object that reminds the fetishist of his sexual partner. The object may be a hat, a lock of hair, a piece of lingerie, etc.
- A body part, such as hair, a hand, earlobe, or neck, that provokes sexual excitement in the fetishist, but is not directly connected with the sexual act.
- Any ritual that the fetishist must perform before or during sex in order to achieve sexual gratification. The ritual might be hair cutting or shoe polishing.

In the late nineteenth century psychiatrists considered fetishism to be a form of masochism. This theory was based on the assumption that all foot and shoe fetishists "deep down" want to be stepped on, walked on, kicked, or otherwise trodden upon. It was believed that they sought both psychological and physical abuse. Even if the shoe fetishist obtained gratification simply from staring into shop windows, what he *really* wanted was abuse, the Victorian psychoanalysts contended.

By the early twentieth century that view had changed. According to English psychologist and author Havelock Ellis (1859–1939), writing in 1906, the fetishist might be viewed in some ways as an exaltant symbolist: ". . . for the masochist his self-humiliating impulses are the symbol of ecstatic adoration; for the foot-fetishist his mistress's foot or shoe is the concentrated symbol of all that is most beautiful and elegant and feminine in her personality." To his mind, this "perversion" could certainly involve masochistic activities, but it wasn't necessarily masochistic.

While the theories have gone through successive changes from one century to the next, the habits of the fetishists have remained pretty much consistent. And whatever the experts' theories, the case histories of fetishists make interesting reading on their own.

Restif de la Bretonne (1734–1806)

Possibly the earliest recorded case of shoe fetishism involved a French novelist named Restif de la Bretonne. Restif used shoes to enhance sexual experience or, in the absence of a partner, as aids to masturbation. In his autobiography, *Monsieur Nicolas*, he reported that his fascination with women's shoes and feet may have begun as early as the age of four, when he first remembered noticing the feet of the opposite sex. By the age of nine, he began watching girls in earnest. He was most attracted to young ladies who were scrupulously clean. He judged their cleanliness—and apparently their sexual merit— by examining their shoes. As he explained in his book, "The part least easy to keep clean is that which touches the earth."

In the eighteenth century women's shoe fashions were frilly and feminine. In Restif's hometown women's shoes were tied with blue or rose ribbons, which matched the skirts of their wearers. The ladies who wore these traditional styles tended to be robust, capable young women. Since Restif by his own description was "frail and weak," he was quite put off by these ladies. He longed to find a woman he could "subdue."

At the age of ten he met a young girl from out of town who was more his match. She was extremely delicate and diminutive. Unlike the local belles, she wore fashionable shoes with buckles and "was a charming person besides." Her beauty, however, was marginally important to Restif, since her feet were unusually attractive. "This taste for the beauty of the feet was so powerful in me that it unfailingly aroused desire and would have made me overlook ugliness." He never managed to make a direct overture to the girl, however. He was too shy.

Restif's modesty, in fact, was almost as strong a force as his obsession with shoes, and the combination of the two occasionally caused him some discomfort. Entering a girl's home he would see her boots arranged in a fastidious row. This made him "tremble with pleasure" until he came face to face with the girl who owned the boots, at which point he blushed violently and lowered his eyes, if he didn't flee altogether. One day he noticed a very pretty pair of shoes in a local bootmaker's shop. He couldn't resist asking who owned them, but when he learned that they belonged to a girl he'd long admired, but never had the courage to approach, he nearly fainted.

At the age of fifteen, Restif was only slightly bolder. He still couldn't directly confront the women to whom he was attracted, but he did manage to steal their slippers and shoes, which he then used in order to masturbate. This established a pattern that accompanied him for the rest of his life.

When he was eighteen, Restif met his ideal woman. She was the wife of a printer to whom Restif was apprenticed. She was young, attractive, delicately built, and had tiny feet and a wonderful collection of shoes. Her slippers were white, green, and rose-colored. Some had silver flowers. Conveniently, Restif lived in the printer's house, so he often had a chance to watch "Madonna Parangon," as he called her, changing her shoes. One day he saw her wearing a pair of rose-colored shoes with tongues, green heels, and a rosette over the toe. He watched her change out of these shoes, then waited until she'd left the room. As soon as she was gone, Restif pounced on her shoes. "I seemed to see her and touch her in handling what she had just worn; my lips pressed one of these jewels, while the other, deceiving the sacred end of nature . . . replaced the object of sex. . . . The warmth which she had communicated to the insensible object which had touched her still remained and gave soul to it; a voluptuous cloud covered my eyes."

Restif's foot fetishism reached its climax during the months he spent with his "Madonna." After he left her home he continued to be fascinated by feet and footwear for the rest of his life, but the fascination never became an obsession, nor did it replace his enthusiasm for normal sexual relations. Madame Parangon continued to represent his ideal in women, however—so much so that he requested that her slipper be buried with him after he died.

The Case of C.P.

This case history was described by Havelock Ellis in *Studies in the Psychology of Sex*, written in 1906. Ellis categorized this as a case of erotic symbolism in which the fetish represents a particularly fulfilling relationship in C.P.'s early life.

C.P. was thirty-eight at the time the case was recorded. He was single and heterosexual, though he didn't have sexual relations with women in the usual way. His version of sex was to lie down on the floor and have a beautiful woman trample him.

He traced this particular fetish back to his teen years, when he had a close friendship with a young woman about six years older than he. She was always exquisitely dressed and had dainty feet and ankles. She wore her skirts short enough to show both. When they went out on walks together, C.P. noticed that she liked to crunch things—flowers, grass, straw, leaves—underfoot. One evening when they were alone together, she tried the same move on him. He was lying stretched out on a thick rug in front of a brightly burning fire. She stepped on him as a joke, to show him "how the hay and straw felt." As she stood on him, he first kissed her foot, which was shod in a brown silk stocking and high-heeled shoe, and then guided it to his penis. When she stepped back on him, he experienced his first complete orgasm, and his "distorted sexual focus was set forever."

During the remainder of his youth, C.P. and his young friend repeated this routine whenever they could, sometimes four or five times in a day. She also seemed to enjoy the trampling. C.P. wrote: "She confessed that she loved to see and feel them [her feet] sink into my body as she trod upon me and enjoyed the crunch of muscles under her heel." Although he couldn't be sure of it, he suspected that "orgasm took place simultaneously with her."

When the girl was away from him, C.P. masturbated using her slipper and fantasizing that she was walking on him. The two never even mentioned the possibility of having "normal" intercourse. When he was twenty, C.P. traveled for several years, and when he returned, the woman was married. They never repeated their "walks" together, but C.P. carried on the practice with prostitutes and other partners.

He was very careful in enlisting any woman who was not a prostitute. Sometimes he would spend as much as a year "getting to know" a woman until he felt safe in making his request. When he did ask, he tried to make it sound like a joke or a game. Apparently, he had little difficulty convincing these women to oblige: "I must have lain between the feet of quite a hundred women, many of them of good social position." By his own account, these ladies never would have consented to ordinary sex with him, but they were either intrigued or amused by his peculiar request.

He was attracted to women of regal demeanor and liked them to wear expensive, elegant evening gowns and high-heeled shoes that were either cut low over the instep or strapped across with a T-strap. He was especially fond of very high-heeled black shoes with tan silk stockings, but did not care for boots or "outdoor shoes." He was repulsed by the sight of nude women, women wearing tights, or women wearing red shoes or stockings. He claimed that his aversion to red was so great that he'd become impotent at the sight of red shoes. (So much for Dorothy's ruby slippers!)

C.P. never asked his partners to remove their shoes or any of their clothing, but while being trampled, he asked the lady to lift her skirts just far enough so he could see her feet and ankles. If she lifted the skirt too far—all the way to her knee, for instance—the "effect" would be "greatly reduced."

The fetish didn't entirely replace sexual intercourse for C.P., but it remained his clear preference: ". . . the pleasure is far inferior to being trampled upon. . . ." The comparative difficulty of obtaining the pleasure from just the woman I want has a never-ending, if inexplicable, charm for me."

The Case of A.N.
Havelock Ellis also reported a case of homosexual boot fetishism, in which, he claimed, the fetish symbolizes not a particular person or relationship but the sense of repression and frustration A.N. feels at not being able to express his sexuality. On a more practical level, the fetish served as a convenient substitute for human sexual relations.

A.N. discovered his affection for boots before he was six

years old. Raised in a very religious upper-class English family, he was often left alone as a child in the nursery. He found his entertainment in prowling through the family closets and retrieving one of his father's boots. He'd secretly bring the boot back to his room and put it on, "then tying or strapping my legs together would produce an erection, and all the pleasurable feelings experienced, I suppose, by means of masturbation."

As he cultivated this ritual, he became particularly susceptible to high boots made of polished or patent leather. The sight, smell, or the mere thought of them would set his "sexual passions aflame." He fantasized about becoming a soldier so that he could wear boots and spurs, or an errand boy so that he could wear their patent leather leggings.

When A.N. reached his teens, he recognized that he was attracted to young boys and men rather than women. Because of his strong religious background, however, he never could bring himself to follow through on his infatuations. From boyhood, he was more or less forced to settle for the physical satisfaction he got from his rituals with footwear.

Short Takes From *Psychopathia Sexualis*
In the early twentieth century the German psychiatrist Richard von Krafft-Ebing wrote about numerous cases of foot and shoe fetishism in his book *Psychopathia Sexualis*. His belief that all foot fetishists are either overt or latent masochists has since been discarded by most psychologists, but his work still provides one of the most comprehensive records of this brand of fetishism to date.

The Brothers X
Does fetishism run in a family? According to one of Krafft-Ebing's cases, it *can*, at the very least. The brothers X represented two different types of fetishists. One liked to dress up in elegant women's shoes. The other liked women to walk on him. One was primarily a voyeur and a fantasizer. The other preferred physical contact.

The voyeur traced his fascination with shoes back to his childhood, when he first began dressing up in women's clothes for masquerade parties. By the time he reached his teens, he was hooked on leather: "The sight of an elegant boot on the foot of a girl at all pretty intoxicated me. I inhaled the odour of the leather with avidity." He wore leather bracelets while masturbating so that he could smell the leather. He dreamt of "shoe scenes" in which he was either gazing into the window of a women's shoe store or lying at a woman's feet while smelling and licking her shoes.

Krafft-Ebing offered no additional information about the second brother's habits, but he did mention that the pair also had an uncle whom they believed to be a foot fetishist.

The Sadomasochism of Shoe Fetishism

Krafft-Ebing described several cases of shoe fetishism in which extreme pain was an essential component of sexual satisfaction. In one case the fetishist was moderately excited by the sight of women's shoes, particularly black leather boots that buttoned up the side and had very high heels. He was happy enough if he could touch, kiss, or wear the shoes, but he was most pleased if he could drive nails through the soles and then walk in them. Although this man also liked to have women walk on him, there's no mention of whether he got the same pleasure if these women had nails protruding through their soles while doing so.

Another case is more overtly sadistic. The fetishist combined his taste for elegant women's shoes with a preoccupation with slaughter. During intercourse he fantasized about his mate's shoes and how animals had died in order to produce the leather for these shoes. Occasionally he would take a live chicken or other small animal to a prostitute and have her step on it while wearing elegant shoes. His name for this was "sacrificing to the feet of Venus." He also liked women to walk on him, (presumably) in order to enhance his fantasies about the death throes of these animals.

Finally, there are the foot lickers. One man would give brand-new patent leather shoes to prostitutes, then lead them through piles of manure and mud before licking the shoes clean. Another habitually licked the feet, which he preferred to be unwashed, and sucked the toes of his partner during intercourse while simultaneously encouraging her to threaten torture if he failed to clean her feet thoroughly.

Barefoot Fetishists

Just as some shoe fetishists are repulsed by the sight of a bare foot, some foot fetishists are interested only in the naked foot, and beyond that they may have even more specific requirements. One homosexual described in *Psychopathia Sexualis* was attracted only to the bare feet of tramps and farm laborers. He followed men on the street who he thought might take off their shoes for him. In order to heighten his fantasy of bare-footedness, he went barefoot himself in even the stormiest weather.

Another man, a middle-aged bachelor, was enthralled by the sight of children's and women's feet. He was from an upper-class "high society" background, however, and few of his female friends were willing to bare their feet to him. Forced to turn his attention to women who ordinarily went barefoot, he spent hours watching the local gypsies or farm laborers. Unfortunately, his high-bred background left him with a keen distaste for *dirty* feet, so he was never completely satisfied.

The Cure

Since the psychologists of the last century viewed fetishism as a perversion, if not a disease, they triumphed whenever they succeeded at "curing" one of their cases.

Krafft-Ebing describes a case of a young man who was fourteen when "a weakness for women's boots came over him." He dreamed of being kicked and tortured. He used boots in order to masturbate, and when he first tried to have normal intercourse, he was impotent. By the time he was thirty he'd had women perform an assortment of masochistic acts with him in the hope of overcoming his impotence. All failed. Finally, he decided that he'd have to overcome his shoe habit if he was ever to have a successful sex life with women.

He bought himself an elegant lady's boot and set aside time each day to confront it. He'd kiss it and caress it, all the time asking himself, "Why should I have erections when kissing this boot, which is after all only an ordinary piece of leather." It was a simple question, but he had a hard time coming up with a logical answer. Eventually, that "ordinary piece of leather" began to lose its charm.

At the same time he was having his conversations with the

boot, the soon-to-be-cured fetishist was trying to have sexual relations with a woman whom he'd instructed "under no circumstances" to submit to his masochistic requests for beating or other physical abuse. For a while after he began losing interest in ladies' shoes, he was dependent on masochistic fantasies, but with persistence he finally managed to establish his virility without any of his former props.

Women Shoe Fetishists

The late nineteenth- and early twentieth-century experts had little to say about women shoe fetishists. They speculated that women did have fetishes, but that they were quite different from men's. There certainly was nothing egalitarian in Krafft-Ebing's view of the situation: ". . . it will be found that the mental superiority of man constitutes the attractive power where physical beauty is wanting." But speculation of the whys and wherefores aside, the real reason these men knew of so few female fetishists was that they didn't treat women. "Details will come to our knowledge only when medical women enter into the study of this subject," wrote Krafft-Ebing, excusing himself from the issue.

Havelock Ellis was more open-minded on the issue. He suggested that some of the women who eagerly participate with men in shoe-fetish rituals must themselves be fetishists. Why else would they keep coming back for more? Ellis also referred to a case of a woman who had "a certain uncontrollable fascination for shoes." This lady had an insatiable appetite for new shoes, which she proudly displayed along with the rest of her collection in a prominent location in her apartment. Even more suspicious, however, was the fact that she changed shoes every three hours.

Some women go to such extremes in order to obtain shoes that they mark themselves as marginal fetishists at the very least. Case in point? We've heard of a pig farmer's wife in the deep South who lives in a shack some 150 miles from the nearest town. Despite poverty and isolation she's managed to accumulate over 300 pairs of elegant shoes. She keeps her shoes in spotless condition and proudly shows them off to all her visitors, which is how we came to hear of her *and* her shoes.

THE FETISHIST'S DREAM SHOES

Restif de la Bretonne

"Her shoes, made in Paris, had that voluptuous elegance which seems to communicate soul and life . . . shoes of simple white drugget, or with silver flowers; sometimes rose-colored slippers with green heels, or green with rose heels."

Richard von Krafft-Ebing

"The fetichist . . . prefers boots with high heels to boots and shoes of a particular kind—buttoned or laced."

C.P., aged thirty-eight

"She must be richly dressed—preferably in an evening gown, and wear dainty high-heeled slippers, either quite open so as to show the curve of the instep, or with only one strap or 'bar' across."

Anonymous male masochist

"My outfit was completed by 5-inch black spike heels."

Mr. X, age twenty-five

"I stand before the show-window of a shoe shop regarding the elegant ladies' shoes—particularly buttoned shoes."

The case of Mr. Z, age twenty-eight

"Laced boots with high heels charmed him most."

The case of X, 1886

"Sight alone was sufficient for him in the case of elegant shoes—i.e., shoes of black leather, buttoning up the side and having very high heels."

| Case 76, *Psychopathia Sexualis* | ". . . he would buy her the handsomest pair of shoes made of patent leather, under the condition that she would put them on immediately." |
| A.N., age twenty-nine | "The sight, or even thought, of high boots, or leggings, especially if well polished or in patent leather, would set all my sexual passions aflame, and does yet." |

Footwear Eros
Erotic Shoe Rituals in History and Art

We've all heard the term "playing footsie" used to describe the secret courtship ritual of touching toes and cuddling feet under the table. Most young lovers do it. Children in school do it. The nineteenth-century American psychologist G. Stanley Hall claimed that even donkeys play a kind of footsie, with the male nipping at his partner's hooves just before mating. Fetishists aren't the only ones who enjoy playing with shoes and feet.

The foot plays a major role in erotic play throughout the world. In addition to studying donkey play, Hall also conducted research that showed that young men and women rank feet as the fourth sexiest part of the body, after eyes, hair, height, and size. Novelists and writers, including Casanova, Thomas Hardy, and Goethe, praised the sexual attraction of a beautiful woman's foot. More recently, in Kurt Vonnegut's *Cat's Cradle* characters make love by putting their feet together, a practice called bacamaroo. Drinking champagne from a woman's slipper has been a standard literary image since the Middle Ages, when the practice was considered a mark of gallantry and admiration. And in some cultures women's feet have been granted such erotic potency that removing a woman's shoe is treated as a crime of passion.

Some cultures actually mandated the covering of women's feet by law. In Spain, in the time of the painter Velázquez (1599–1660), the Catholic Church insisted that the Virgin's feet be covered in all religious paintings. Monarchs and nobility were given the same treatment. When a local manufacturer dared offer the queen a pair of silk stockings, the gift was quickly rejected with the explanation, "The queen has no legs!"

Prostitutes worldwide have found ways to use their feet in attracting as well as entertaining their clients. In ancient Rome prostitutes were not allowed to wear the closed shoes worn by other women. Instead, they wore gilded slippers. The shining footwear and the naked toes served as a walking advertisement for the profession. Some Spanish prostitutes bare their feet as a signal of assent to their clients. And high spike heels, of course, are a standard accessory for prostitutes in virtually every major Western city today. Most Western prostitutes may not use their shoes as major props in the bedroom, but they know the value of a sexy shoe when it comes to attracting business.

In some societies the foot is treated as a cultural fetish. Among tribes in Siberia and eastern Russia, it is considered obscene for a woman's feet to be uncovered, even if she is otherwise naked. In some of these cultures the bride and groom remove each other's stockings as a nuptial ritual symbolic of intercourse.

In China before Mao Tse Tung gained power, the adoration of women's feet was raised to a national obsession. Women's feet were granted the same sexual value among the Chinese that women's breasts have among men in the Western world. Centuries of pornographic engravings show men fondling women's naked feet. Chinese prostitutes perfected positions in which they used their feet to fondle and manipulate their partners' genitals. Chinese men described the experience as the ultimate aphrodisiac. The size of the foot was considered more important than a woman's face as a measurement of beauty. Because of its erotic significance, it was considered highly improper for any man but the husband to look at a woman's feet. The earliest reports of Chinese footbinding date back to about 1100 B.C., when the country was ruled by the Empress Taki, who had a club foot. It is said that she instituted the practice of swaddling women's feet in order that all women might resemble her. This was only a temporary practice, however, and did not survive the empress herself.

China's national foot fetish, on the other hand, did persist. The rejuvenation of footbinding during the early Sung Dynasty (A.D. 960–1279) was a grotesque outgrowth of that fetish. The Sung rulers first instituted footbinding among dancers of the royal palace. The bound foot became known as a lotus foot and was thought to enhance a woman's sexual powers, even to promote the development of the thighs and sexual organs. It also accentuated women's subservience to men and, by effectively crippling them, branded them as members of the leisure class who didn't have to perform physical work. Scholarly men grew foot-long fingernails to prove the same point.

From the palace dancers the practice spread to women throughout China, with the exception of nuns, slaves, prostitutes, and certain peoples, such as the Manchus. The heavy bandages were first applied when a girl was as young as three or four years of age. The big toe was pressed inward, the other toes bent underneath the foot. The constant pressure from the bandages and the restriction of circulation combined to shorten the foot to as little as three inches.

It was taboo to ever remove the bandages before a man's eyes, and most women wore them to their graves. There are tales of women committing suicide after their bare "lotus feet" were viewed by men.

The bandages also helped support the foot, since the binding prevented any development of muscle or normal bone support. Women wore trousers with bindings at the ankle to strengthen their ankles and hide the sticklike legs that were another side effect of footbinding.

The seeds of change were cast by the last empress of China, Tz'u Hsi, at the turn of the twentieth century. As a Manchu, the empress did not have bound feet. When she opened a school in Peking for the daughters of nobility, she forbade entrance to any girls who had bound feet. The exclusionary rule spread to other private schools of the day, and the upper classes began to be persuaded to change their ways.

Foreign missionaries also campaigned against the custom. In 1895 Protestant ladies formed the Natural Foot Society and sent a petition to the empress to outlaw footbinding. The empress had no objection, and she wanted to win favor with the foreigners, so she passed an edict against the custom in 1902.

Despite these efforts the Chinese old school continued to look upon unbound feet as a sign of poverty and ill-breeding. With the increasing power of the Communists, these old schoolers clashed with women revolutionaries, who arrived in the large cities wearing sandals hand-fashioned out of straw and string. The more flamboyant of the young women attached pompoms and tassels to the footgear, but all wore them with bare feet. Their objective was to demonstrate their sympathy for the laborers and peasant classes, but the sandals and the women's bobbed haircuts caused such cries of outrage among the traditionally minded Chinese that many of the revolutionary leaders backed off slightly and began wearing cloth shoes or rubber tennis shoes, which at least covered their feet.

With the creation of the Republic in 1911, footbinding was outlawed once and for all. The custom of almost a thousand years had been cast aside within a single generation. In China today the only remaining women with "lotus feet" are in their seventies or older. No doubt there still are Chinese men who mourn the passing of this ultimate foot fetish.

The Shoe in Marriage

Ancient Eastern European Customs

The shoe served as a symbol of a man's marital state. A man without a shoe was either married or unfit for marriage; a man with both shoes was a potential suitor to the single woman.

During the wedding ceremony the bridegroom handed a slipper to his bride in order to indicate his domination within the marriage. When the bride put on this slipper, she symbolically conceded that she had become his subject. When a man died, his widow took the shoe of her brother-in-law to indicate that he could not marry her.

Middle Eastern Customs

After discarding a wife, the Arab Bedouin recites, "I have thrown away my slipper." This officially terminates the marriage.

Among both Arabs and Jews, and also in many parts of Europe, it's customary for the groom to give shoes to the bride and to various members of her family, often including the bride's mother and sisters.

Among Palestinian Jews, it's important that the bridal slipper fit perfectly so as to ensure that the bride and groom "fit" perfectly in marriage. For this reason, the groom sends a shoemaker to the bride's home. On the day of the cobbler's visit, the couple sets the date for their wedding.

Chinese Customs

Shoes and the cloths used to bind the bride's foot were an essential part of the bride's dowry. The bride made the shoes herself, and there were usually at least six pairs in the dowry. One red bridal shoe was tossed over the roof of her house to ensure happiness. She might also be required to give shoes to her new husband's mother, grandmother, and sisters.

The shoes and the bride's foot, if it was especially tiny, were on display for friends and family. The bride proved how tiny her foot was by measuring it against a 2-inch spoon. If the bride's foot was too large, everyone would ridicule her and her new husband's family.

Russian Custom

Russian peasants had a ritual in which boots were used to determine the fate of young couples who wished to marry. The father secretly placed a handful of oats inside the son's boots. He then instructed the son to bring him the boots one after the other. If the son brought the boot with the oats first, the father consented to the wedding. If the empty boot was brought out first, it was considered a sign that the marriage too would be barren, reason enough for the father to oppose the union.

Western Customs

Along with rice, many people believe in throwing slippers after departing couples on their wedding day. The tradition stems from an Anglo-Saxon custom in which the father of the bride symbolically transferred authority over the young woman from himself to the groom by giving the groom a shoe belonging to the bride. (In some places, however, the practice is frowned upon. It was outlawed, along with the throwing of rice, according to a local edict in Portsmouth, Ohio, in 1913.)

Today's bride and groom celebrate their wedding vows with two old shoe customs. One stems from the rhyme "Something old, something new, something borrowed, something blue, and a penny in your shoe." The other calls for a train of old shoes to be tied to the newlywed couple's getaway car.

Footwear Insights

How Shoes May Be the Key to Your Lover's Personality

"Whenever I meet someone for the first time, I always look first at his shoes. You can always tell what a person is like by looking at his shoes." The fashion editor who delivered this comment isn't the only one who thinks there's more to shoe fashion than meets the feet. Popular life-style pundits recently have created formulas for determining a person's true personality by examining his feet. Good-bye tea leaves, hello shoes!

- *Sneakers:* A man who wears sneakers and bounces on his feet tends to jump from one woman to the next.*
- *Black oxfords:* Men who wear sensible shoes are smart, but boring. They plod through life the same way they plod down the street.
- *Wingtips:* Men who lace themselves into formal shoes tend to be controlling and emotionally distant.
- *Brown penny loafers:* The penny men are at least one woman's version of prince charming.

*These and other opinions by Diana Katcher Bletter, *Glamour* magazine, March 1983.

The ultimate "funny-looking" sandal is the Birkenstock. Margot Fraser is the founder of Birkenstock Footprint Sandals, Inc., the company that imports the German sandals to the United States. In 1984 her company grossed $7 million by ignoring fashion.

Courtesy of Birkenstock Footprint Sandals, Inc.

HIGH SOCIETY

AS TIME GOES BY

All fashion designs begin as sketches. For footwear manufacturers and buyers, these sketches are essential because they provide a glimpse of the next season's ready-to-wear clothing. The manufacturers and buyers use this information to make their own sketches of next season's shoe designs. These sketches reflected some official fashion predictions for 1985.

Illustrations by Aleta for the Footwear Council.

During the seasons when patterns are "in," they can seem to be the only element that sets one shoe apart from the next.
Courtesy of the Footwear Council. © 1984 by James Dee Daley.

Andrea Pfister combines crocodile, lizard, and snake for a boot and matching bag in his 1983 collection.

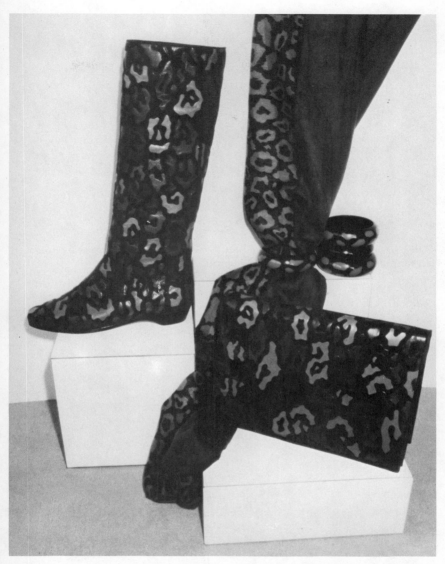

In another boot-and-bag combo Pfister uses imprinted leather reminiscent of zebra and ocelot for an exotic look.

The fairy queen has cast her spell on these lacy evening pumps by Stuart Weitzman, who designs for Mr. Seymour and Martinique.
Courtesy of Stuart Weitzman.

All that glitters is not . . . These subtly striped creations by Stuart Weitzman are "paved" in rhinestones.
Courtesy of Stuart Weitzman.

French designers, like Thierry Mugler, cater to upscale boutiques in the United States that go out of their way to avoid trendiness.
Photograph by Donna Cline.

The Japanese designer Kenzo recently has begun designing footwear. He joins the ranks of other clothing designers—Norma Kamali, Yves St. Laurent, Gloria Vanderbilt, Liz Claiborne, Geoffrey Beene, Ralph Lauren, Perry Ellis—who also design footwear.

Courtesy of Kenzo.

Edwin Moses, only one of the many athletes who endorse a brand-name footwear, holds up his Adidas in triumph at the 1984 Los Angeles Summer Olympic Games.
Courtesy of Adidas.

A jogger's security totem. This shoe keychain was produced during the peak of the running boom in the early 1980s.

Million-dollar boots? Tony Lama calls them the "El Rey III." This one-of-a-kind pair of cowboy boots is studded with precious gems and metals. Although fit for a king, these boots have never been worn. They are for display only.
Courtesy of Tony Lama.

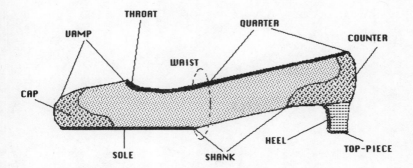

THE PARTS OF A SHOE

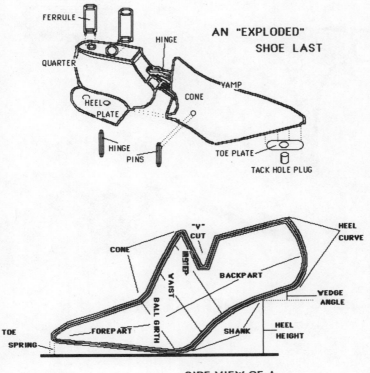

AN "EXPLODED"
SHOE LAST

SIDE VIEW OF A
SHOE LAST

THE PARTS OF A SHOE LAST

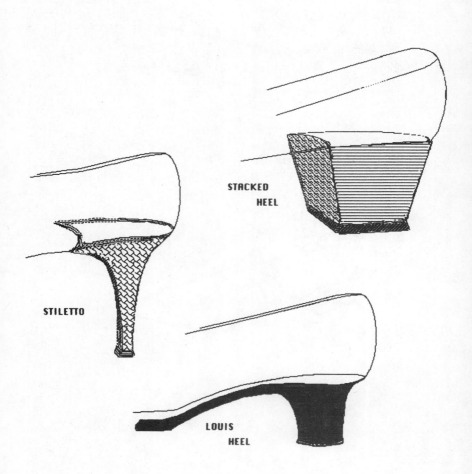

STACKED
HEEL

STILETTO

LOUIS
HEEL

HEEL STYLES

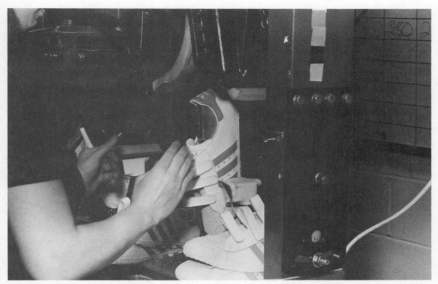

The stitched upper is stretched onto a last and the fiberboard inner sole is attached.
Courtesy of Adidas.

Heat and pressure are applied to the shoe on the last to give it shape, and glue is applied to the bottom to receive the outer sole.
Courtesy of Adidas.

Creative packaging is one way of getting more mileage in footwear marketing. The Los Angeles importer L. A. Gear created a specially designed box to match a single shoe style. The duo was especially eye-catching in store displays.

Courtesy of L. A. Gear.

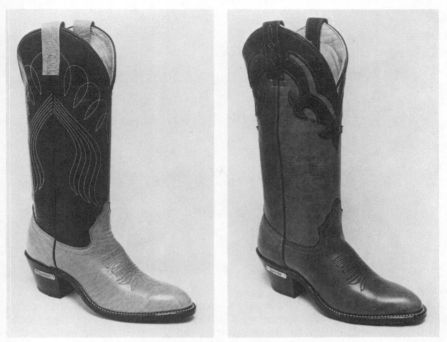

Today's cowboy boots for the urban fashion plate.
Courtesy of the Footwear Council.

Boots for boys in action, fall 1984. Clockwise from lower left: desert boot with ribbed bottom by Buster Brown; foul-weather boot with fleece lining, leather shaft, and molded rubber foot by Sperry Topsider; hiking boot with padded collar and tractor bottom by Kinney; hiking boot of suede and nylon with ridged bottom by Hush Puppies.
Courtesy of the Footwear Council. © 1984 by James Dee Daley.

The fashion boots of fall 1984 hearken back to the leggings of Robin Hood with earthy colors and textures and a soft fit. From top: wrapped loden boot with combined textures by Thorn Brown; banded boot of suede with stacked heel by Nickels; speed laced bootie of suede by Mootsie's Tootsies.
Courtesy of the Footwear Council. © 1984 by James Dee Daley.

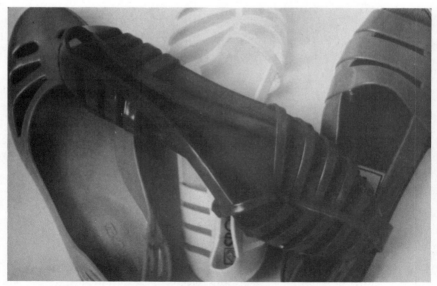

Jellies: a short-lived, low-cost shoe fad.
Courtesy of the Footwear Council. © 1984 by James Dee Daley.

Two slides and a slingback, all variations on the mule. Clockwise from left: semi-d'orsay slingback platform with cork wedge by Jazz; mule, or slide, with cork bottom by Footworks; mule, or slide, with cork bottom by Golo. Courtesy of the Footwear Council. © 1984 by James Dee Daley.

The pump dresses up for the 1984 holiday season. Clockwise from center: sequined pump with satin toe and heel by Anne Klein; slingback pump in metallic and velvet by Garolini; low-heeled pump of satin with gem-studded heel by Geoffrey Beene; low-heeled pump with gem-studded vamp by Stefania. Courtesy of the Footwear Council. © by James Dee Daley.

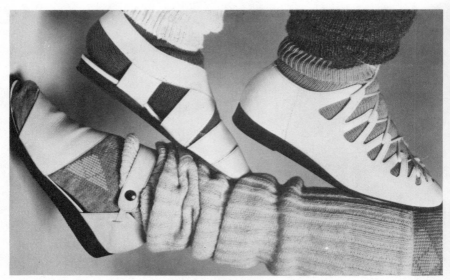

Winterized sandals worn with wooley leggings in 1984. From top: closed gillie by Seven Star; strippy sandal by Ripa; ankle-strap sandal by Buckray. Courtesy of the Footwear Council. © 1984 by James Dee Daley.

Women aren't the only ones who desire a closet full of shoes. Children are also the target of marketing efforts to sell a barnyard full of sneakers. Zoo Shoes offers animals—from doggies to ducks—for the little set. Courtesy of Zoo Shoes.

Athleisure has become *the* look for teen and post-teen rockers. Flexible and casual, these reborn sneakers have arrived on high school campuses and city streets.

Courtesy of L. A. Gear.

"Sophisticated lady" has a new meaning in the 1980s. She's turned into the rebel without a cause. Unconstructed and surprising from the toes up, this decade's fashion plate is as comfortable in army boots as evening glitter.
    Courtesy of Leon Max.

Courtesy of Electra Casadei.

FOOTWEAR FOR FEATS *

FOR MOUNTAINEERING
HanWag's "Expedition" ($275)

FOR WHITE WATER RAFTING
From Teva Sierra ($27)
Designed by river guide Mark Thatcher

ROCK CLIMBING
Fine' ($79)

KAYAKING
From Tabata ($56)
Worn by the American team that
made the first descent of the Karnäli River, Nepal

*Source: **Outside Magazine**
September, 1984
Prices Approximate

DOWNHILL SKIING AND TOURING
From Han Wag ($250)
A cross-purpose, two boot-in-one
combination ski boot with an inner boot
that lifts out for skiing

TRIATHLONING
From Power Sports ($12)
There's no single shoe yet that will work for
all the sports in a triathlon (biking,
swimming, and running) but these
sandals will work between sports -
and massage your feet, to boot!

REEF AND HOT ROCK WALKING
From Patagonia ($18)
They're actually Japanese fishing sock-boots,
but their synthetic soles will save your feet
from both slippery rocks and hot rocks,
whichever's your pleasure!
They're great for white water
rafting, too.

SKATEBOARDING
Van's "Off The Wall"
Van Doren Rubber Company ($42)
Also a candidate for dirt biking

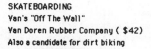

BOARDSAILING
Alpina ($40)
Adhesive, wraparound soles grip
the board to prevent you from
slipping into the surf

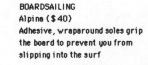

ICE CLIMBING
From Koflach ($250)
High tech plastic for climbing
to the peaks of the world

IVAN LENDL COLLECTION

adidas

Olympic specials. With the start of the 1984 Summer Olympics in Los Angeles, footwear manufacturers went all out to promote specialized footwear for sports of all varieties. Adidas was one of the major contenders in this battle for the spotlight, with Olympic season shoes for tennis, parachuting, and a spike-studded shoe for sprinters. Adidas claims the sprint shoe's system of adjustable spikes and other "adjustable elements" offers the athlete a choice of 62,705,664 possible combinations on each shoe.

Courtesy of Adidas.

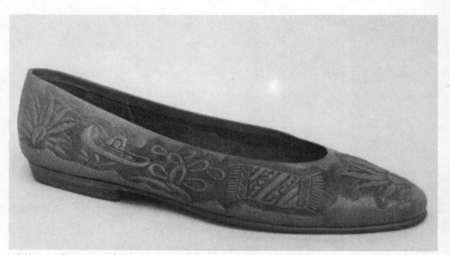

Chilis, a division of Impo International, established in September 1985, took its name and its look from the Southwest flavor of the embossed shoes from Mexico. Here a popular teen shoe silhouette is combined with pictures to tie into a revived western look.

Courtesy of Chilis.

THE HUMAN FOOT

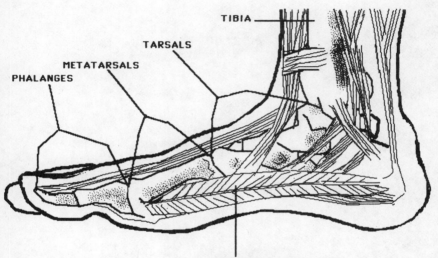

TIBIA

TARSALS

METATARSALS

PHALANGES

PLANTAR LIGAMENT

The Adidas Shoe Museum, West Germany.
Courtesy of Adidas.

An early leader in the alternative lacing game was Kaepa, a firm based in San Antonio, Texas. The split-vamp, two-lace system was devised by the company founder, Tom Adams, after he discovered that his tennis shoes became more flexible and comfortable if he used two separate laces to secure the upper and lower sections of the vamp. The original shoe is in tatters now, but you get the idea.

Courtesy of Kaepa, Inc.

4

SHOES BY DESIGN

The Origins of Style
Backtracking Through Today's Footwear Attitudes

Some trends in fashion cannot be charted by fashion forecasters. These trends evolve because of a quirk in history, an economic crisis, a cultural revolution, or some other societal shift. Some last just a few weeks or months, while other styles span several generations. Here are the stories of some major trends in footwear fashions that have swept the nation in the last few years.

Athleisure
It all started during the New York transit strike of 1980. Career women were walking miles to and from work each day in their fashionable high heels until both their feet and shoes began to fall apart. A new trend was born when pedestrian commuters discovered the joys of walking to work in athletic shoes (and sensibly *carrying* those painful pumps to wear after arriving at the office). It didn't take a genius to figure out that walking in sneakers is easier than in 3-inch heels, and by the time the

transit strike ended, the sports shoe–business suit statement was firmly established.

The footwear industry soon caught on to the public's desire for shoes with both comfort and fashion. Designers responded by combining athletic shoe function with the form of leisure shoes, like espadrilles, and athleisure made its entrance into the world of footwear fashions.

Since that time, athleisure has come into its own, with everyone from Nike to Charles Jourdan making the shoes. The looks range from the revamped tennis shoes of the fifties to sleek jazz oxfords in smooth leather with polyurethane soles. But while shoe manufacturers have embraced the style, most persist in rejecting the name, insisting that theirs are "true casuals."

Preppy

It seems as though campus coeds on the East Coast have been squeezing into plaid skirts and shetland sweaters with circle pins for as long as anyone can remember. Those classic tweeds, plaids, and pinstripes were made to go with tailgate parties and homecoming football games. They are also comfortable and functional. But each few years the nuances of prep are revised as the next generation of college fashion plates lines up for orientation. When the preppy look surged to the fashion forefront in the fall of 1980, it had been revised from its last nationwide heyday back in the seventies.

The 1980 preppy wore loafers, oxfords, and deck shoes. Sperry Topsiders, espadrilles, flat pumps, and penny mocs completed the mandatory footwear code. Preppy women adopted the look of little girls wearing frilly dresses and Mary Janes, suede-bowed ballet slippers, or silver wedges. The authentic preppy of 1980 could be clothed entirely out of the L. L. Bean catalog.

One new element in the preppy mix was jogging. Ivy Leaguers discovered running and the accessories of running. Crocodile-studded warm-up suits and high-priced athletic shoes became *de rigueur* both on the tracks and off.

Although the preppy look subsided somewhat after 1980, it made a comeback again in 1985. Man-tailoring characterized this new edition for both men and women, with cable-knit sweaters, blazers, argyle socks, chinos, and kiltie slip-on shoes. Campus casuals, watch out!

The Era of the Pump

Pumps are a perennial favorite, and they made a serious dent in the fashion pages in the early 1980s, when the economy dictated a more conservative direction in politics and clothing. But neither manufacturers nor consumers were willing to settle for unadorned pumps. Variations on the theme included slingbacks, open toes, d'orsay sides, shelled-out flats, and high stiletto heels. Comfort was critical in this generation of pumps, however, and the lower heel heights became the best-sellers. To spark up these low-lying shoes for evening, manufacturers bejeweled them with rhinestones and sequins, sleeked them down with feathers, and cut them daringly low across the toes.

The simplicity and versatility of the pump took hold. Today, nearly half of the 400 million shoes sold in America each year are pumps. This is one shoe style that's recession-proof.

Indian Mocs

Indian mocs have been going to summer camp for many moons, but until recently they never went any further. Some Boy Scouts actually made their own traditional version with deerskin or calfskin fringe and embroidered bead trim. Others waited for the field trip to a nearby Indian reservation to buy their mocassins.

In the last few years the moccasin has expanded its image and spun off versions ranging from high heels to open thongs. The consistent features are soft leathers and outer stitching. Fashionable additions include woven leathers, smoothed-down lasts, and metallic finishes. Late in 1984 a moccasin appeared on the scene festooned with costume jewels. The moc had gone funky.

Whatever Happened to Birkenstocks?

"If you're goin' to San Francisco . . . be sure to wear flowers in your hair . . ." So went the refrain of a generation nationwide. But those who were actually *in* San Francisco at the time were wearing Birkenstock sandals on their feet as well as flowers in their hair.

Birkenstock sandals are those funny-looking shoes that burst onto the hippie fashion scene around the time of the student unrest on the Berkeley campus in the late sixties. The sandals are made in Germany by a family-owned business that dates back to 1774, the year John Adam Birkenstock was registered as a shoemaker in the church archives. Around the turn of the twentieth century, Conrad Birkenstock conceived the notion of a contoured sole that fit the shape of the human foot. Two more generations of Birkenstocks refined and developed this idea into today's Birkenstock sandals.

These shoes have an inner sole that resembles a footprint. It molds to the feet, evenly distributing body weight. The sandals are so lightweight and comfortable that they give the wearer a "barefoot on the beach" feeling even when walking on hard surfaces.

The sandals were introduced in this country by Margot Fraser, a forty-year-old housewife who discovered the shoes during a trip to Europe in 1966. Three months of sightseeing in Birkenstocks cured her aching feet and turned her into a believer.

When Fraser decided to import the sandals, the hippie movement did not figure into her plans. She started out by taking samples to shoe stores, but the response was so dismal that she was forced to take alternative action. "It was obvious that these shoes had to be sold by people who believed in the concept of healthy shoes," she recalls. "So I went to a health food fair."

Fraser managed to convince a few health food stores that the shoes would sell if given a chance. She was right. The sandals suited a generation protesting war and middle-of-the road values. They fit with worn blue jeans, work shirts, and long hair.

In the eighties fashions have changed. Students now wear prim skirts, slacks, and even ties to class. Rebels who formerly warned against "trusting anyone over thirty" are now working on Wall Street and having babies. The Yippies (Youth in Protest) are now Yuppies (Young Urban Professionals), but despite all these changes, some of them still are wearing Birkenstocks on their feet.

In an industry where styles change weekly, the Birkenstock sandal has remained the same. The distinctive footprint sole maintains its reputation for comfort, and the Birkenstock market extends from South Africa to Norway. In the United States the sandal's largest following still lives in the San Francisco Bay Area. The flower people may be old news, but the Birkenstock sandal is alive and well in northern California.

Birkenstock's celebrity clientele includes

Congresswoman Bella Abzug
Psychoanalyst Erik Erickson
Actress Carrie Fisher
Actor Harrison Ford
Heptathlete Jane Fredrick (inspiration for the motion picture *Personal Best*)
Franciscan monks
Actor Larry Hagman
Actress Goldie Hawn
Beach Boy Alan Jardine
Apple Computer's Chairman Steven Jobs
Psychiatrist and author Elisabeth Kübler-Ross
Baseball pitcher Bill Lee
Actor Don Meredith
Actress Cybill Shepherd
The Smothers Brothers, comedians
Basketball star Bill Walton
Actor Dennis Weaver

One Step Ahead
The Process of Plotting Fashion Trends

Have you ever wondered why last year's accessories never seem to work with this year's fashions? Who decides which heel height works and which doesn't? Is there some sort of conspiracy that changes the dye lots *just* enough so that last year's shoes don't match this year's bag? Or is there a cyclical formula that dictates fashion comebacks every seven or eight years (just long enough for most of us to have turned over the contents of our wardrobes at least once, throwing out the very styles that are destined to make a comeback)?

In fact, there *is* a conspiracy, of sorts, and there is also a general pattern to the rotations of fashion. The core conspiracy is made up of color designers who work with fiber and textile companies. These designers determine which colors and textures will be "important" more than two years in advance of a given season. After they've mapped out their chosen color combinations, the textile companies distribute this information through subscriber services to tanneries and fabric mills. The leather and textile designers then pick and choose among the available selection. *Their* final choices are based on market factors, such as what sold the previous season and to whom. For example, if gray was "important" last year, it probably will return with a hint of purple or green to set it apart this year. If the couturier set was enchanted by gold last year, then gold will be pushed on the mass market this time around.

Some industry fashion analysts claim that there's a seven-year cycle in fashions, which accounts for the rise and fall and rise again of hemlines, heels, pastels, and glitter. But this pattern is far from absolute. As one leather house designer explains, "I call them like I see them . . . and if I don't see them, I make them up."

Once the color charts are made up for a particular season, they're sent to the manufacturers. The color designers bolster their case with in-person seminars, and the leather companies display their latest wares at their semiannual trade show. Footwear manufacturers consider the available materials in light of their projected styles. Will their proposed flats look better in tan or burgundy? Will the lines of their new evening shoes be more sensational in metallic or flat textures? When the manufacturers have committed their orders for materials, the designers go to work fine-tuning their lines. They make drawings and specify colors. Patterns are cut and samples made. Information about the new styles is "leaked" to the fashion publications, which filter and distill the reports into "trends."

Fashion editors frequently play as large a role in creating these trends as they do in reporting them. Always on the lookout for new sensations, an editor of *Vogue, Glamour,* or *Women's Wear Daily* may glimpse a young girl's neon bracelet or a scarf wrapped haphazardly around a skier's boot, then blend the two images to come up with a completely manufactured fad: the neon-wrapped boot. She calls on the manufacturers to help her illustrate the improvised trend: "I'm doing a spread on wrapped neon boots. Have you one for us to shoot?" Even if they've never heard of wrapped neon boots, most manufacturers will instantly produce an appropriate sample (in a fashion model's standard size 8 or 9 rather than the shoe sample size 6) if it means having *their* shoe featured in a national consumer publication.

By the time the national shoe industry trade show begins, nearly every manufacturer and importer in the country has at least one wrapped neon boot plus every other style that's featured in the fashion magazines. The buyers for retail stores attend the trade show with the intention of ordering merchandise for the next season. Watching one another carefully, they narrow the selection of colors and styles for their particular markets. Retailers from Los Angeles and New York will be looking for new, hip styles for America's capitals of fashion. Midwestern buyers will concentrate on the looks that sold on the coasts last year, since consumers in the midsection of the country follow more conservative purchasing patterns. But even with the geographic variations, the fashions that figured most prominently on the pages of the magazines will probably sell out everywhere. Whether they like it or not, most consumers accept the fact that fashion is dictated *to* them rather than *by* them.

THE TREE OF SHOE DESIGN

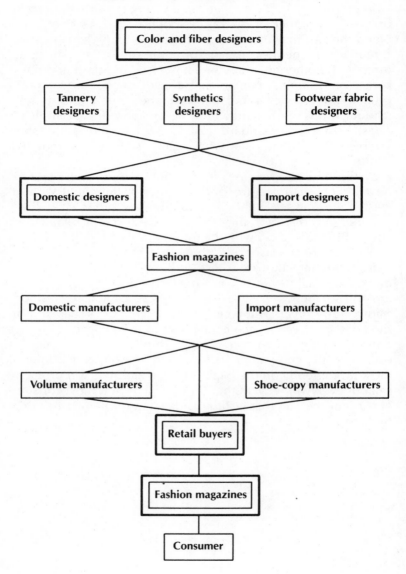

DESIGN TIME LINE
SPRING 1986–SPRING 1988

April 1986	Fiber color designers select spring colors for 1988
Summer 1986	Textile services distribute color information for 1988 to fabric and leather companies
October 1986	Leather designers begin to develop colors for 1988 leathers
January 1987	Leather companies debut 1988 leathers at industry trade show
February 1987	Footwear designers begin to work on shoe styles for 1988
March 1987	Shoe companies begin to manufacture 1988 spring line
June 1987	Shoe companies show the 1988 line to retailers for the first time
August 1987	Retailers place orders for shoes for spring 1988
December 1987	First 1988 spring shoes arrive at retail stores
May 1988	Clearance sales begin on shoes designed for spring 1988

The World's Leading Footwear Designers
Who They Are—What They Like—How They Work

Maud Frizon

Perhaps the most famous female shoe designer in the world, Maud Frizon is as flamboyant as her design creations. This former fashion model owns real estate from the chateau country of France to Manhattan's Madison Avenue. She and her husband, Luigi de Marco, commute between their apartments in New York and Paris and their sprawling 370-acre country estate in the Loire Valley via a fleet of vehicles that includes three BMWs, a Bell Jet Ranger Two helicopter, and a 70-foot boat named *Maud,* which they keep anchored in the harbor of Venice, Italy. They also own 23 prize-winning horses.

Maud Frizon's shoe factory, located near Venice, employs 300 craftsmen, who turn out approximately 150,000 pairs of handmade shoes each year. The United States accounts for 35 percent of her market, with the rest spread throughout the world. The average retail price for a pair of Maud Frizon shoes is $90.

Luigi de Marco handles the financial and marketing affairs of Frizon's footwear business. Because he negotiates sales without the use of intermediaries, the company works on a substantially larger than average profit margin. Operating profits on Maud Frizon shoe sales are estimated to be about 25 percent, a successful percentage in any business.

Andrea Pfister

Andrea Pfister was born in Pesaro, Italy, in 1942, then moved with his family to Switzerland, where he attended school. Back in Italy as a university student, Pfister studied art and languages in Florence before selecting his professional goals. In 1962 he attended the Ars Sutoria Shoe Design School in Milan, and in 1965 he presented his first shoe collection bearing his own label. His shoes attracted the notice of such trend-setters as Catherine Deneuve, Cher, Barbra Streisand, Candice Bergen, Ursula Andress, Monica Vitti, and Claudia Cardinale. Within ten years he had his own factory and had established a life-style that incorporated a villa on the Italian Riviera, scores of celebrity friends and customers, semiannual visits to the United States, and travel throughout the world.

Pfister's primary design concerns are color and leather, followed in priority by the proportions of the last and heel styling. While still a student, Pfister won first prize in the Shoe Designer International Contest in Amsterdam. His shoes today are reproduced under license in Japan, Turkey, Spain, and South America. The shoes are sold in boutiques throughout the world.

Andrea Pfister's villa perches on the rocky mountainside along the Amalfi Coast, just below the resort village of Positano. Named Torre della Gavitella after its square Saracen tower, the villa dates back to 1100. Pfister himself designed his salt-water pool, furniture, and the terra-cotta tiles lining the surrounding terraces. The villa is a regular stopover for Pfister's many renowned friends, including the writer Gore Vidal, the film director Franco Zeffirelli, the composers Henry Mancini and Quincy Jones, and the actor Ben Gazzara.

Yves St. Laurent

Every world-class fashion designer has his or her own unique work habits, but Yves St. Laurent is the only designer to have his own shoe studio. The studio helps him guarantee the quality and integrity of design in his licensed footwear line.

Every Yves St. Laurent shoe begins as a drawing by Yves St. Laurent himself. The drawing then goes to the shoe atelier in his Paris offices on Avenue Montaigne. Here a staff of five, headed by Monsieur Alexandre Narcy, translates the designer's two-dimensional impression into a three-dimensional prototype. First the studio selects the last that will shape the shoe. The heel is created from the studio's own molds, and patterns are cut first in paper, then leather. The leather patterns are then stitched and nailed to the last before the soles and heels are attached.

The completed prototype is sent to the Yves St. Laurent footwear factory in Rossimoda, Italy, to be transformed into samples. The sample shoes are then sent back up to Paris for final review by Yves St. Laurent. If he approves, they're sent to the United States licensee, Schwartz & Benjamin, for sale and distribution.

Roger Vivier

Ask Roger Vivier what adjectives best describe his shoes and he'll promptly reply "simple" and "extravagant." But not everyone would so easily categorize this designer's more than 4,000 creations spanning five decades. The shoes range from flats, which Diana Vreeland once described as "flat as tongues," to pumps with needlelike metal heels.

The designs satisfy the fashion tastes of millionaires, movie queens, and royalty. Vivier's following includes such notables as the queen of England, Elizabeth Taylor, Helene Rochas, Marlene Dietrich, Claudette Colbert, the duchess of Windsor, the empress of Japan, and five Rothschild baronesses. Diana Vreeland prized her collection to the extent that she instructed her maid to polish the soles and treat the leather uppers of her Vivier shoes with rhinoceros horn.

Now in his late sixties, Vivier continues to design footwear at his medieval castle, the Chateau d'Aubeterre, nestled in the foie gras and truffle country of France's Aubeterre-sur-Dronne region. His down-to-earth work area is just about the only "simple" area in his home. The rest caters exclusively to his craving for "extravagance."

From his countless journeys around the world, the designer has brought home artifacts ranging from African carvings and Oriental sculptures to Cycladic art and Egyptian statues. The walls are lined with eighteenth-century tapestries, the floors with seventeenth- or eighteenth-century carpets from Europe and the Orient. Interspersed are modern paintings by such artists as Hans Hartung, Jacques Villon, Robert Delaunay, and Georges Rouault.

Vivier began his love affair with the art world while a student at the École des Beaux Arts in Paris. His goal was to become a sculptor. He was sidetracked into his future profession by chance, when he began designing shoes for family friends who owned a small shoe factory. By the time he was in his early twenties, Vivier had joined forces with the designer Elsa Schiaparelli to bring platform shoes to the forefront of the fashion world. He had his own atelier on the Rue Royale in Paris and sold designs to Bally in Switzerland, Pinet in France, Salamander & Stiller in Germany, Rayne in Great Britain, and I. Miller and Delman in America. The American market eventually lured him into exclusivity, however. Delman brought him to

New York and kept him exclusively until 1947, when Vivier switched gears by teaming up with the millinery designer Suzanne Remy and opening the most fashionable hat shop in Manhattan, called Suzanne & Roger. After the war Vivier returned to France and to shoe design. Some years later he would again design exclusively for an American salon, this time at Saks Fifth Avenue, but his home would remain in France.

Vivier is best known in fashion circles for his alliances with couturier clothing designers. He was the first footwear designer to present shoe designs in twice yearly collections during the presentations of couture wear. He is the only footwear designer with whom Christian Dior would share a label.

Today Roger Vivier shoes are sold in France through the Durer boutiques. In addition to his own label, Vivier designs for the Thierry Mugler collection. He also has, for the first time, his own retail stores in New York and Paris. His ambition seems to intensify with age. By his own admission, "I am going to prove that I am stronger than ever."

Ironically, what has not changed over the years is Vivier's casual attitude toward the shoes he wears on his own feet. No custom designs for this designer. Just plain Italian loafers. He may labor over the styles that suit his female clientele, but when it comes to his personal footwear, "I really don't think about what I put on my own feet."

Andre Perugia

Andre Perugia, probably the most renowned shoemaker in the world, was introduced to the elegant Parisian clientele at the age of twenty by the magician of haute couture, Paul Poiret. Perugia became an artist in the sphere of shoemaking, the most famous of his century, with a clientele of such illustrious women as Garbo, Marlene Dietrich, the Queen of England, and Eva Perón. Perugia designed no fewer than 180 pairs for Perón, the first lady of Argentina and possibly his most difficult customer.

In 1962, the designer joined ranks with Charles Jourdan, leaving him the business three years later in order to retire. To the rest of the world he left what might be the most valuable collection of shoes in existence, displayed at the Charles Jourdan Museum in Romans, France.

When the museum made a U.S. tour in 1984, officials of the

company refused to reveal which shoes had been worn by celebrities. They explained that in a previous tour certain "labeled" shoes had been stolen from the priceless exhibition.

The collection highlighted changes and movements in footwear history during the twentieth century. They included cork-wedged sandals in cloth or raffia from the days of wartime rationing, the heavy platform heels of the 1930s and 1940s, the egg-shaped toes and shapely heels on dancing shoes from the 1920s, and the stylized pointed "winkle-picker" or "needle nose" of the early 1950s.

Andy Warhol distinguished the collection with a poster designed for the tour.

WORLDWIDE DESIGNER RUNDOWN*

DESIGNER	LABEL
Andrea Assous	Andrea Assous (formerly Jacques Cohen)
Marc Alpert	Marc Alpert Maria Pia
Arsho Baghsarian	Arsho Shoe Biz
Geoffrey Beene	Geoffrey Beene Beene Bag
Susan Bennis	Warren Edwards
Polly Bergen	Polly Bergen Polly B.
Dorothee Bis	—Freelance—
Mario Bologna	Bologna & Figli
Ottorino Bossi	Vigevano
Moya Bowler	Biarritz
Roger Bowman	Martegani
Salvatore Capezio	Capezio

*This is a partial list only. Stores are listed alphabetically, not by rating.

DESIGNER	LABEL
Pierre Cardin	Pierre Cardin for Men
Bart Carlton	Mia
Oleg Cassini	Oleg Cassini
Liz Claiborne	Liz Claiborne
Robert Clergerie	Robert Clergerie
Jacques Cohen	Jacques Cohen
Betty Dorn	Mootsie's Tootsies
Perry Ellis	Perry Ellis
David Evins	I. Miller
Reed Evins	Two City Kids
Melissa Evins	
Joe Famolare	Famolare
Beverly Feldman	Beverly Feldman Nickels
Salvatore Ferragamo	Ferragamo
Fiamma Ferragamo	
Silvia Fiorentina	Fiorentina
Adreano Fosi	Golden Street
Peter Fox	Peter Fox
Maud Frizon	Maud Frizon
Jean-Paul Gaultier	—Freelance—
Andrew Geller Family	Andrew Geller
	Sleekers by Geller
	Strada by Geller
	Julianelli
Guerino	Monique of Vigonovo
Joan and David Halpern	Joan & David
	David & Joan
Renée and Mickey Harrison	J. Renée
Miguel Hernandez	MHS collection
John Higdon	John Higdon
Mabel Julianelli	Julianelli
	Andrew Geller
Charles Jourdan	Charles Jourdan

DESIGNER	LABEL
Norma Kamali	Norma Kamali
Donna Karan	Anne Klein
Jim Katz	Zodiac
Stephane Kelian	Stephane Kelian
Calvin Klein	Calvin Klein
Nancy Knox	Nancy Knox
Ralph Lauren	Ralph Lauren
Brian Lennard	Sacha
Herbert and Beth Levine	Andrew Geller
Marco Martini	Castelfranco di Soto
Paul Mayer	Paul Jeffries
Mary McFadden	Mary McFadden
Maggie Mercado	Pappagallo
Jerry Miller	Shoe Biz
Nolan Miller	Dynasty Collection
Margaret Clark Miller	Margaret Jerrold
Thierry Mugler	Thierry Mugler collection
Walter Newberger	Walter Newberger for Wilkes Bashford
	Testoni
	Walter Chase
Albert and Pearl Nipon	Albert Nipon
Martini Osvaldo	Martini Osvaldo
	Martini Moda
	Boutique Marco
	Harve Bernard
Andre Perugia	Charles Jourdan
Andrea Pfister	Andrea Pfister
Elliot Pliner	Elliot Pliner
Vittorio and Alberto Pollini	Alberto Pollini
Todd and Evelyn Ricci	Divertente
	Vittorio Ricci
Renzo Rossetti	Fratelli Rossetti

DESIGNER	LABEL
Yves St. Laurent	Yves St. Laurent
Fausto Santini and Alvaro Dominici	Santini & Dominici
Elisabeth de Seneville	—Freelance—
Bill Valentine	Bill Valentine Collection Amano D'Antonio Stanley Philipson John Jerro
Martinez Valero	Martinez Valero
Gloria Vanderbilt and David Siskin	Gloria Vanderbilt
Roger Vivier	Roger Vivier Thierry Mugler collection Christian Dior & Roger Vivier Delman
Stuart Weitzman	Mr. Seymour Martinique
Zalo	Paradox by Zalo

A Buyer's Guide to Shoe Paraphernalia
Footwear Accessories, Past and Present

There's more to footwear than shoes; there are shoe *accessories*! The following mini-catalog offers a glimpse of footwear addenda available throughout history.

Musical Soles
The ancient Greeks liked to make music wherever they went, so they invented shoes called *kroupeza*, made with music-making soles. The sole was split underneath the toes to accommodate a metal wind pipe. Depending on the pressure and angle of the footstep, the pipe would play a tune as the wearer walked or danced.

Brass Boot Protectors

Another version of musical shoes was created by a London shoemaker in 1817 with the invention of brass boot protectors. The shoemaker's clients were more taken with the noise the thin brass plates made on the cobbled streets than they were with any functional qualities of the invention. In fact, they gloated to such an extent that they created the following ditty:

> *Both Learned and Dunces are vain, it is said*
> *(Each in turn oft betrays what he feels),*
> *And they who no notice can gain by their head,*
> *Make a noise in the world with their heels.**

These simple brass plates evolved into the drilled horseshoe-shaped cleats and taps that still punctuate the drone of city streets and high school hallways.

Shoe Studs

The catalog description reads: "It's just like having studded tires for your shoes!" The device instantly turns your favorite pair of walking shoes into a no-slip version of golf shoes. The tungsten carbide studs are mounted on an all-rubber sandal unit that slips on over your shoes to allow you to walk on ice.

Shoeshine Valet

Professional shoeshiners have a broad array of equipment, including special chairs, shoeshine boxes, and stools, but the shoeshine valet is only for the most elite of shoeshiners. It allows you to keep your shoes in tiptop gloss without straining your back and legs. The adjustable aluminum shoe holder has one expandable end that fits inside your shoe (up to size 13). The other end slides into a wall-mounted bracket. Depending on where you mount the bracket, you can stand or sit while shining your shoes. The valet will hold the footwear still as you apply paste and polish.

If the Shoe Fits—Eat It

That's the name of a chocolate shoe that was introduced in time

---

*Thomas Wright, *The Romance of the Shoe* (London: C. J. Farncombe, 1922).

for Christmas 1982. The product was billed as a "good natured truce offering for someone who has a habit of saying the wrong thing at the wrong time." Here was a foot that was intended to be put in your mouth. The 4.3-ounce shoe was packaged in a small blue box and came with its own plastic knife.

Shoe Warmers
Remember tea cozies and toaster covers? Now there are shoe warmers for the faint-hearted among L. L. Bean's loyal mail-order following. Shaped like little feet, these stoneware forms are placed first into the oven to warm and then into your shoes or boots to toast them up on chilly mornings.

Boot Trees
Custom boots can be a heavy investment, and boot trees can make the difference in preserving expensive and unique boots. One company that understands the importance of shape in a boot is Tony Lama. For that reason, Tony Lama sells its own brand of Bootrees made of plastic and aluminum and designed to hold the instep up and the boot toe down. The trees sell for about $5 a pair in most Western shops.

Rain Booties
"Good news for bad weather." They're called rain booties, and they fit over high-heel shoes of all sizes to ward off splashes of water and mud. These plastic sleeves zip up the front and have an elastic opening for heels. For the stylish touch, they come in yellow, black, taupe, or transparent plastic with nonskid soles and a scalloped collar. "Tough wearing, feminine looking," trumpets the manufacturer Nora Nelson. "Tiptoe through the raindrops."

Foot Forms
Shoe stores use them to display shoes. Shoe and foot fetishists possess them as totems. They're the models used to support footwear in shop windows and on display counters. Among the classiest versions available are the foot forms manufactured by the Bernardo Shoe Company, Columbus, Ohio. They come as right or left feet, flat or lifted heels, with toes parted slightly to allow the wearing of sandals (Bernardo is primarily a sandal

manufacturer). If you want the higher price version, you can order the Logo Foot, a Bernardo signature model with a sandal sculpted on. The Logo Foot comes in antique gold.

"Health Shoes"

Magnetic acupressure footwear has arrived in Peking, China. The shoes are now being tested as a possible cure for high blood pressure, nervous exhaustion, and insomnia. They look like standard-issue cloth Mary Janes, but the soles contain two to four permanent magnets, each measuring a third of an inch in diameter. The magnets are positioned beneath sensitive points on the sole of the foot. Theoretically, the magnetic field triggers these pressure points to send signals to the nervous system to relieve pain. Out of 340 volunteers in China who tried the shoes, 300 reported "very impressive recoveries."

Stinky Pinkys

The natural answer to smelly sneakers was invented by the PDZ Corporation. Stinky Pinkys are mineral sachets that "take the stink out of sneakers overnight." After three months of continuous use, they get a bit tired, but they can be revived by a day out in the sun and fresh air. The cost? Just $5.95.

Air Shoes

To add a lift to their step, many athletes today wear air shoes. The soles of these shoes contain a one-way valve leading into the heel chamber through which air is pumped. Air pressure can be adjusted as in a tire, from 1 to 4 pounds, with a small pump that comes with the shoes. Some air shoes have soles made of blown sponge rubber with two connected air chambers. Others have separate air bladders, which slide in as inner soles. Air shoes range in price from $50 to $100.

Design-A-Boot

The Grizzly Boot Company, located in Anaconda, Montana, dares you to be choosy by offering you the chance to design your own personalized work boot or cowboy boot. In work boots, your styling choices include a selection of sole materials, heel shapes, toe styles, dimensions, and internal supports. Your choices in designing your own cowboy boots include toe and heel styles, stitching patterns, leather types, design shaping, and additional decoration. The Grizzly Boot Company specializes in boots for the "man's man" professions, with specific boot styles for loggers, smoke jumpers, linemen, ranchers, and snow shovelers. Prices run anywhere from $160 for the basic cowboy boot to more than $800 for an ostrich skin Prairie Hen cowboy boot. For the ultimate in service, this mail-order company also offers a full line of hardcore footwear accessories, including replaceable caulks, hardened steel spikes that screw into the soles of boots; utility plates, hardened steel plates that fasten to sole edges to protect boots against abrasion caused by climbing poles (assuming you're a lineman); Tricounis, Swiss-made steel grip plates that fasten to the outer sole of the boot for extra traction when walking timber; boot hooks, steel hooks with "comfy" wooden handles that slip through cowboy-boot straps to help pull the boots on; miner's toe guards, steel caps mounted over the outside of the boot toes to protect them through a hard day in the mines; and elk antler belt buckles, adorned with the head of your favorite "critter" (the look is natural, the coating pure acrylic; these one-of-a-kind buckles require a special order).

Shoelaces Save Lives!

Your child's life just might be saved by his or her shoelaces, *if* you use the Lifesaver Info. cards produced by a company called Finn Products. The cards are small rectangles of heavy-duty cardboard with a hole through which to string them onto your child's shoelaces. The cards have spaces for all vital identification and medical information, including allergies, special medication, blood type, and insurance carrier. The card also provides a space for the parent's signature permitting surgery to be performed should it be necessary and the parent cannot be reached.

Computer Shoes

For the truly dedicated runner, Puma has developed the ultimate pedometer—a computerized running shoe. At the time of purchase, the customer performs a simple calibration exercise from which the shoe's inner computer assembles the information it needs to measure the distance, pace, and caloric expenditure for each subsequent run. The runner activates the shoe by using a weatherproof button at the start of each run. If desired, the shoe will bleep loudly when the runner achieves a preset distance. After the run, the shoe plugs into a home computer and charts out the distance, time, speed, and calories burned. It will also provide a graph of the weekly or monthly progress. Adidas also has its own version of the shoe.

For Shoe Snobs Only

Where can you find $67,000 worth of shoes designed by Maud Frizon? Where is shopping for Oscar de la Renta and Russian sables a game? Just when you thought you'd finally memorized all the answers to Trivial Pursuit, along comes a game that picks your pocketbook instead of your mind. Called SNOB, the $45 board game challenges players to be the first to spend $10 million on a fantasy shopping spree from soup to shoes. The game follows in a long line of shoe games dating back to the first horseshoe toss and the creation of the little metal shoe on the Monopoly board.

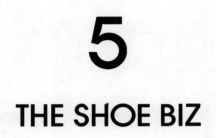

5

THE SHOE BIZ

What comes to mind when you think of shoemakers and shoe salesmen? Chances are, you *don't* think of conglomerate businesses and millionaires. Yet the shoe biz *is* a multibillion-dollar industry that spans every continent and makes many of its members extremely wealthy.

What once was considered a fairly low-level trade has become, by virtue of industrialization and mass marketing, an intensely competitive profession. The independent shoemaker is a member of a rare and vanishing breed, who now, by virtue of his scarcity, has turned into a "custom shoemaker" entitled to command a price astronomically higher than he ever could have expected in an earlier era. The larger manufacturers, on the other hand, are constantly developing ways to enhance the quality of their products so that they are *better* than handmade.

Fashion trends and life-style shifts, such as the running boom, have created an insatiable market for footwear, which, in turn, has transformed essentially entrepreneurial companies, like Nike and the U.S. Shoe Company, into industrial giants. The success potential filters down through the ranks even to the salespeople at your local shoe stores, who may earn $100,000 or more in a single year.

In the following pages we'll give you a crash course in the footwear industry—how it works and who makes it jump. We'll even tell you the *real* stories of the names behind the labels.

Footwear Best-sellers
What the Hits Are and How They Make It to the Top

Just as there are best-selling books, so there are best-selling shoes, which grab the fancy of the footwear market and fashion world for a season or so before fading from sight. For a glimpse of the buying and selling habits within the American shoe world, take a look at the following facts and figures, representing the highlights of one spring and summer season.*

MEN'S FOOTWEAR FACTS

FOOTWEAR BEST-SELLERS

SANDALS: Double-straps and thongs
DRESS SHOES: Loafers and moccasins
CASUAL SHOES: Oxfords
ATHLETIC SHOES: Running shoes
SLIPPERS: Classic opera and plain closed-back styles

KEY FACTORS IN PURCHASING SHOES
(RATED IN IMPORTANCE FROM 1 TO 5)
1. Quality
2. Service-delivery from manufacturer
3. Fashion-style
4. Comfort-fit
5. Price

TYPICAL OPENING DATES OF SPRING FOOTWEAR
CLEARANCE SALES
DEPARTMENT STORES: June 1 through June 20
INDEPENDENT STORES: June 21 through July 10
CHAIN STORES: June 21 through June 30

*Fairchild Publications, N.Y., *Footwear Survey Men's and Women's Shoes,*
Spring 1982 Season.

BUYING HABITS OF MALE SHOE SHOPPERS
1. On the average, 60 to 70 percent actually make a purchase when shopping.
2. The average shopper buys just one pair at a time.
3. The average purchase in dollars:
    DEPARTMENT STORE: $110
    INDEPENDENT STORE: $ 85
    CHAIN STORE: $ 53

WOMEN'S FOOTWEAR FACTS

FOOTWEAR BEST-SELLERS
SANDALS: Open-toe–open-heel slingbacks and thongs
DRESS SHOES: Slingbacks and open-toe pumps
CASUAL SHOES: Espadrilles
ATHLETIC FOOTWEAR: Running shoes
SLIPPERS: Open-toe slides and washable scuffs

KEY FACTORS IN PURCHASING SHOES (RATED IN IMPORTANCE FROM 1 TO 5)
1. Fashion-style
2. Quality
3. Price
4. Service-delivery from manufacturer
5. Comfort-fit

TYPICAL OPENING DATES OF SPRING FOOTWEAR CLEARANCE SALES
DEPARTMENT STORES: May 1 through May 31
INDEPENDENT STORES: June 21 through June 30
CHAIN STORES: July 1 through July 10

BUYING HABITS OF FEMALE SHOE SHOPPERS
1. On the average, 60 to 70 percent actually make a purchase when shopping.
2. The average shopper buys two pairs at one time.
3. The average purchase in dollars per pair:
    DEPARTMENT STORE: $32
    INDEPENDENT STORE: $40
    CHAIN STORE: $37

Who's Whose Promo Pick
Footwear's Athletic Hall of Fame

The following is a partial listing of the key athletic spokespersons for major athletic footwear manufacturers, past and present.

COMPANY	EVENT	ATHLETE
Adidas	Olympic track and field	Jesse Owens (Olympic decathlon champion, 1936—wore shoes made by Dassler, owner of Adidas) Bob Beamon (long jump) Ralph Boston (long jump) Ed Burke (hammer throw) Jurgen Hingsen (decathlon) Edwin Moses (hurdles) Dilly Olson (pole vault) Wilma Rudolph (track) Daley Thompson (decathlon)
	Baseball	Cal Ripken, Jr. (Orioles)
	Basketball	Kareem Abdul-Jabbar (Lakers)
	Boxing	Muhammad Ali
	Football	Eric Dickerson (Rams) Joe Montana (49ers) Herschel Walker (Jets)
	Marathon	Ron Clarke Grete Waitz

COMPANY	EVENT	ATHLETE
	Soccer	Franz Beckenbauer Fritz Walter
	Tennis	Ivan Lendl
Nike	Basketball	Moses Malone (76'ers)
	Track	Mary Decker Slaney Carl Lewis China's Olympic team
	Marathon	Joan Benoit Alberto Salazar
	Tennis	John McEnroe
Converse	Olympic track and field	Ron Brown (track) Mike Conley (long jump) Earl Jones (track)
	Baseball	Ron Kittle (White Sox)
	Basketball	Larry Bird (Celtics) Julius Erving (76'ers) Earvin "Magic" Johnson (Lakers) U.S. Olympic teams since 1936
	Football	Tony Dorsett (Cowboys)
	Marathon	Paul Cummings Julie Isphording Arthur Lydiard
	Tennis	Jimmy Connors Chris Evert Lloyd
Asics Tiger	Olympic track and field	Jeanette Bolden (track) Dwight Stones (high jump)

COMPANY	EVENT	ATHLETE
	Olympic gymnastics	Kathy Johnson
		Julianne McNamara
		Mary Lou Retton
		Tracee Talavera
		Peter Vidmar
	Marathon	Juma Ikanga
		Alison Roe
		Toshihiko Seko
	Olympic wrestling teams	Britain
		Canada
		China
		Japan
		United States

PERCENT OF RUNNING SHOE MARKET
BY MANUFACTURER BRANDS

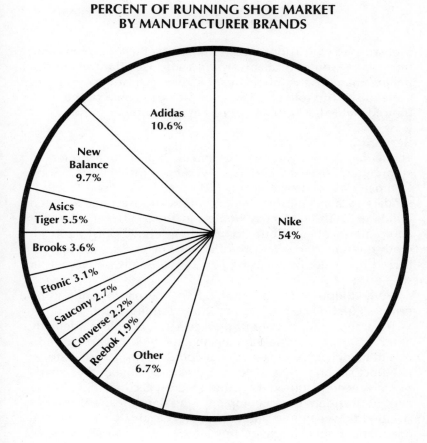

Who's Who in Shoes
The Faces Behind the Labels

Ever wonder who Thom McAn is or where Buster Brown came from? If so, you're probably in for a surprise. The true stories behind many of the labels in shoes we wear are novel, if not outlandish. The following sampler includes some of the most unpredictable background stories in the footwear trade.

Bernardo

The name is synonymous with sandals, but it actually refers to an architect, Bernard Rudofsky, who gave the Bernardo Shoe Company its start back in the 1930s. Rudofsky "constructed" sandals in a geometric fashion, the same way he designed buildings. Although most women in the 1930s considered it immoral, or at best risqué, to bare their feet, Rudofsky considered the human foot a work of art worthy of display. He publicized his belief by focusing his magazine ads on women in sexy poses.

While Rudofsky designed the original Bernardo sandals, the firm was first owned by Eva and Nino Sonnino, who had their own flamboyant ideas about publicity. The couple particularly liked to create exotic sandals that were both artistic and breathtakingly expensive and that could be displayed in stores to attract shoppers to the Bernardo name. Some of these early sandals recently toured the United States, accompanied by the current president of the company, Matt Barouh. The diamond-studded flower thongs and coiled-snake sandals still drew the press and public. Perhaps the interest was keener because Bernardo now is known almost exclusively for stripped-down thongs and casual shoes that are the antithesis of those first outrageous styles.

Bostonian

Charles H. Jones had a certain image of himself. Even though his factory was located in Whitman, Massachusetts, he still considered himself a Bostonian at heart. So in 1884, when he incorporated his business to become the Commonwealth Shoe & Leather Company, he seized the opportunity to change the label in his men's shoes from Charles H. Jones shoes to Bostonian shoes. Their nickname, "the gentleman's shoe," has stuck to this day.

Buster Brown

The original Buster Brown was a cartoon character created in 1902 by Richard Fenton Outcault. Buster was an early version of Dennis the Menace. Dressed up as Little Lord Fauntleroy, he appeared in the comics alongside his sister, Mary Jane, and his dog, Tige. These three characters, patterned after Outcault's own son, daughter, and pet dog, were as popular in their time as Little Orphan Annie and Charlie Brown were for later generations.

Buster Brown became the trademark for a line of children's shoes in 1904, when the Brown Shoe Company (named for the founder, George Warren Brown, and not for Buster) purchased rights to the name from Outcault. At the St. Louis World's Fair that year, the Buster Brown shoe brand was introduced to the public, but it was soon overshadowed by a host of other Buster Brown products. Outcault himself set up a booth at the fair and proceeded to sell off trademark rights to the name for products ranging from harmonicas to apples. The price for the name reportedly ranged from $5 to $1,000, depending on the cartoonist's inclination.

Shortly after the fair, there were more than fifty products named Buster Brown, but the Brown Shoe Company got more marketing mileage out of the trademark than any other licensees. Between 1904 and 1915, and again between 1921 and 1930, the company sent out midgets dressed like Buster to promote the shoes. Accompanied by Tige-like dogs, they performed in theaters, department stores, and shoe stores across the country.

In 1943 Buster made it to the broadcast media with the debut of Smilin' Ed McConnell and his Buster Brown Gang. Ed and the Gang moved into television in 1951, and stayed there until Ed's death in 1954. The actor Andy Devine replaced Smilin' Ed, but the show remained on the air only one more year.

Of all the products that carried Buster Brown's name back in the early 1900s only Buster Brown shoes and a line of textiles remain today. John A. Bush, the young sales representative who cajoled the company into buying the name back in 1904, received just rewards. In 1915 he became president of the company, and in 1948, chairman of the board.

Capezio

Like most early American footwear companies, Capezio began as a shoe repair shop. Salvatore Capezio had immigrated to America from Italy at the turn of the century and opened his store in the heart of the New York City theater district near the Metropolitan Opera House. His clientele was made up almost exclusively of performers.

The story goes that Salvatore began making shoes almost by default. An opera singer who had misplaced his costume shoes came to the cobbler in a panic, and Capezio made him a new pair in time for that evening's performance. As a result, the entire Metropolitan Opera company began ordering custom-made footwear from the Italian shoe repair man.

Capezio acquired his reputation as a shoemaker for the ballet when the Russian ballerina Anna Pavlova arrived in this country for the first time and asked him to make a collection of dance slippers for her nationwide tour. Capezio had been making ballet slippers for New York dancers, including his wife, but this order established his name as the most prestigious brand in dance shoes.

In the late 1940s, Capezio was invited to expand beyond the world of the arts and into the world of fashion. The designer Claire McCardell, who specialized in casual, active women's clothing, asked Salvatore to create a complementary line of footwear for her line. He responded with a collection of colorful ballet-inspired flats made for streetwear. These designs caught on across the country and eventually spread into children's footwear fashions as well.

Today, the name "Capezio" is used by two different manufacturers. The dance shoes are still made in New York City by Capezio Ballet Makers, Inc. Capezio fashion shoes are made by a division of the U.S. Shoe Corporation in Cincinnati, Ohio.

Caressa

The podiatrist Leonard Taicher had a vision of the ideal shoe. In his mind's eye he saw shoes that would "caress" the foot. To turn vision into reality, Taicher moved with his wife, Betty, to a villa on a mountainside in Haiti and employed local workers to fashion footwear from sisal and raffia. The result was cool, comfortable, and eventually popular. Production increased from 300 pairs a day until the couple had to move their operations to larger quarters in Miami. Taicher's line also expanded to include styles that were more traditional in appearance, but the ultimate priority of comfort remained. Today Caressa is a division of the U.S. Shoe Corporation.

Clinic

Even accidents can inspire shoes. More than fifty years ago the founder of the Juvenile Shoe Corporation, Chester Reith, flipped his sports car on a Missouri highway. As a result, he spent weeks in a hospital recovering from a broken collar bone and other injuries. The recuperative period gave him a chance to observe nurses in action. He decided they desperately needed special shoes for the long hours spent on their feet. Although the Juvenile Shoe Corporation heretofore had manufactured only children's shoes, Reith began work on a line of duty shoes as soon as he recovered. The line was called Clinic, in honor of the nurses Reith had met during his stay in the hospital clinic.

Jacques Cohen

Who would think that back in the 1960s the king of espadrilles was managing a drugstore! Admittedly, Jacques Cohen was working for Le Drugstore, one of the in spots of Paris, but the fact remains, he knew nothing of the business that soon would make him a millionaire.

Cohen had the inspiration for his gold mine during a trip to America in the heyday of Swedish clogs. He compared the clogs to the espadrilles worn in France and Spain, and in his estimation the espadrilles were superior. He decided to experiment with importing his own slightly modified versions of the Basque footwear.

Cohen met a lukewarm reception from American retailers, who couldn't understand why anyone would buy footwear that was neither shoe nor sneaker and was so incredibly inexpensive that millions would have to sell in order to turn a profit. Finally, Cohen received his first order from Best & Co. for 108 pairs. Each pair cost about $3 wholesale, $7 retail. The rest, some might say, is a miracle of footwear history.

Today, Jacques Cohen Ltd. sells more than a million pairs of shoes a year and has offices in New York, Dallas, Los Angeles, Spain, Taiwan, and Monte Carlo. Cohen himself divides his time between an apartment in Monte Carlo and a villa he recently built in St. Tropez. He shares his residences with his wife, his two nearly grown children, his dachsund (with a pedigree signed by Prince Rainier of Monaco), and his pride-and-joy collection of pre-Columbian Mexican and Peruvian sculptures and paintings. With his empire intact, Jacques Cohen is enjoying the rewards of a gamble played to win.

Famolare

The Famolare name in shoes dates back two generations to the now-defunct pattern-making firm of Famolare Shoe Engineering. Joe Famolare, Sr., founded the firm and was determined to have his son succeed him. The younger Famolare was equally determined "to be a star" in his own right.

Joe Famolare, Jr., set out on his road to stardom by designing shoes first for Capezio and later for Marx & Newman. When he'd satisfied his curiosity about how other firms ran their business, he decided to try his own hand. In 1969, with a modest loan from Wall Street bankers, Joe Famolare started a company that a decade later would generate $100 million of business a year. He was just thirty-eight years old.

Famolare staked his claim on fashionable shoes that are comfortable first and foremost. He won a Coty design award in 1973 for his wood and plastic clog that followed the contours of the foot. In 1975 he introduced a shoe with a thick thermoplastic sole molded into four waves on the bottom. The purpose of the waves was to absorb the shock of walking on hard pavement. Famolare called this the Get There shoe, because it was designed to help you get there. To promote the shoe, he commissioned a song called "Get There," and inserted a record of it in every box of the shoes. He created a dance to go with the song, and encouraged shoe stores to stage dance promotions.

Famolare's formula for success has remained fairly constant from the start. Comfort and fit hold top priority. Next comes durability, and beauty comes in last. Adherence to this formula, however, has brought Famolare both ups and downs. In the mid-1970s his wave-bottom creations were an essential part of women's—and some men's—footwear wardrobes from coast to coast. His celebrity clientele over the years has included Paul Newman, Shirley Jones, Gregory Peck, and Walter Matthau. Such designers as Anne Klein and Givenchy translated his designs into high-class versions for the boutique set. The violinist Isaac Stern commissioned half a dozen custom-made Famolares, including white sport shoes for day and patent leathers for evening performances.

The popularity of his shoes allowed Famolare to build up an empire consisting of retail shoe stores, franchised units, corporate offices in a restored Manhattan townhouse, *and* a 40-acre villa in Florence, Italy, but Famolare has also experienced dips in popularity. In the late 1970s his ripple-soled creations plummeted out of favor with the fashion world's trend-setters. To make matter worse, he came under attack from women's groups because of a 1978 ad campaign that had been devised to spice up the company's "sensible" reputation. The advertisements contained disembodied parts of female models wearing the Famolare shoes. In one ad the model stood next to a man with a gun, intended to look like the starting gun in a race. But the intended message didn't translate visually, and the verbal messages—"High heels don't have to hurt" and "Don't let the streets beat up your feet"—didn't help counteract the undertones of violence. The ad campaign triggered boycotts and pickets.

Famolare fought back with a new line of shoes that were brighter in color and trimmer in silhouette. He also introduced a new ad campaign headlined "Footloose and Famolare." Joe capitalized on his zest for stardom by becoming the primary model in the F and F ads, all photographed by the star maker Richard Avedon. The switch paid off not only in renewed sales but also in praise from the same women's groups who'd protested his earlier ads. Women Against Pornography officially honored him in the spring of 1982 for his switch from "sexist" promotion to "fun-oriented" advertising. Famolare later teamed up with feminist Jane Fonda to create a line of "workout" shoes.

Ferragamo

Salvatore Ferragamo founded the dynasty, and it lives on under the guidance of the Florentine shoemaker's daughter Fiamma. In Italy and throughout the world the Ferragamo name has come to mean style, fit, and quality, and the current generation intends to keep it that way.

The current generation consists of Fiamma, who designs today's Ferragamo shoes, and her five brothers and sisters. Salvatore's wife, Wanda, is still active in the family business, which now includes clothing and accessories in addition to footwear. The Ferragamos continue to base their operations in Florence, Italy, with a showroom that resembles a medieval palace banquet hall. In all aspects of their business, comfortable elegance is the name of the game.

Foot-Joy

Any golfer knows the brand name Foot-Joy, but these golf shoes started out as men's dress shoes back in the 1920s. They were made by the Field & Flint Company, which held a contest among employees to come up with a name for the line. The winning name, Foot-Joy, reflected the image of comfort and ease that the company badly wanted to convey to consumers. It was introduced as a brand in 1925. The golf shoes made their debut in 1927. Today Foot-Joy shoes are manufactured by Foot-Joy, Inc.

Andrew Geller

The name is synonymous with quality classic women's shoes. It's the name of the founder of Andrew Geller Industries, Inc., a seventy-four-year-old company that began as a shoe store on Sixth Avenue in New York City. By midcentury the firm had joined the ranks of the top three fashion footwear companies in New York. It attracted top designers from all over the world and owned six American factories.

Andrew Geller built the company with his brother and partner, Robert. Andrew's son Monroe and Robert's son Bert were given instructions to establish themselves in business outside the company before coming back to the family fold. The young men joined forces to build a rainwear manufacturing company. They married women who were roommates in college. And in the late 1940s they returned to Andrew Geller Industries to steer it into the second half of the twentieth century.

As head of merchandising for the company, Bert instituted a policy of promotional hoopla. He welcomed each new fashion season with high-velocity fashion shows and parties at which he promised "lots of booze" and "no food." One year the magnanimous merchandiser flew a group of retailers cross-country to New York at his firm's expense so they could see the fall collections—both Geller's and every other firm's. The experiment was such a hit with both retailers and fashion houses that they decided to make it a habit. There now is a major footwear fashion show in New York every December to debut the next fall's collections. The company's current brand names include Julianelli, Sleekers, Geoffrey Beene, and Beene Bag, as well as Andrew Geller.

Hush Puppies

Back in the 1950s the Wolverine Company developed a process for machine-flaying pigskins that for the first time made it possible to use pigskin as the primary material in moderate-priced shoes. The company soon took advantage of the situation to introduce a line of comfortable, casual pigskin shoes. A national survey was conducted in order to name the line, and Hush Puppies emerged somewhere midway in the survey. It would have been thrown out but for the efforts of one of the members of the Krause family, which founded Wolverine. The company accepted the argument that the new shoes were capable of "hushing barking dogs" and adopted the name.

Keds

Rubber-soled, canvas-topped athletic shoes first appeared in this country in the 1880s, but the U.S. Rubber Company became the first to introduce a national brand of sneakers in the early twentieth century. The brand was first named Peds, after the Latin root for "foot," but the name was already trademarked. The company then combined the original idea with "kids," who made up the bulk of the market for these shoes, and the result was Keds.

Tony Lama

The founder of one of the leading cowboy-boot manufacturing companies, ironically, was the son of Italian immigrants. Tony Lama, Sr. (1887–1974) grew up not in the deserts of the Southwest but in the northern reaches of New York State. And his education in shoemaking began at the age of eleven, when he began working in footwear factories.

Tony Lama's escape from the cold northeastern climate came with his enlistment in the U.S. Army, which ended at Fort Bliss, Texas. Lama took a liking to the mild weather and a local music teacher, who soon became his wife. The couple settled in the border town of El Paso, and in 1911 Tony Lama opened his original shoe repair shop with the help of a single assistant.

The shop's initial customers were ranchers, cowboys, and members of the U.S. Cavalry. Lama and his assistant repaired boots and put "lifts" in the shoes of the town's ladies. As Lama's reputation grew, ranchers and cowboys brought him hides so that he could make them new boots as well as repair their old ones. He made twenty pairs of new boots his first year, and two decades years later Tony Lama had quit the repair business and turned exclusively to the manufacture of Western boots for ranchers and cowboys. In time the popularity of Western boots spread to the entertainment industry, and Tony Lama products acquired their own celebrity following, including Roy Rogers, Rex Allen, Gene Autry, and numerous Nashville country singers.

Tony Lama's six children all contributed to the growth of the company, which by 1970 included divisions making leather products and Western clothing. His eldest surviving son, Tony Lama, Jr., is chairman of the board of the Tony Lama Company. The youngest son, Louis Lama, is president.

Oomphies

Remember the Oomph Girl? That was actress Ann Sheridan's nickname in the early 1940s. It became the name of a brand manufactured by La Marquise Footwear shortly after one of the Oomph Girl's press conferences in which she was asked what kind of shoes she wore. She couldn't remember the actual brand so she dubbed them Oomphies. La Marquise wasn't about to turn its back on this gift horse. Immediately the name was registered and a logo was created with eyes inside the O's. Miss Sheridan took full credit for the new brand name and received royalties on the shoes for the rest of her life.

Sperry Topsider

Sperry Topsiders today are an essential component of the preppy wardrobe, so it's fitting that they were created by a yachtsman. Paul Sperry never dreamt that he'd enter the shoe business until a boating accident nearly cost him his life in the 1930s. Afterward, he realized that it was folly to slip and slide around boat decks in leather soles. He experimented with designs for shoes featuring nonskid rubber bottoms combined with deck leather uppers. Sperry Topsiders were born. Their creator first marketed them through mail order, which was how Abercrombie & Fitch discovered them. The store became his largest customer. But Sperry had no enduring interest in the shoe business, and ultimately he sold out to Uniroyal. Today Sperry Topsider is a division of Stride-Rite Shoes.

Thom McAn

Key employees at Thom McAn each have their own versions of how the name came to exist. Some are more exotic than others, but as near as we could tell, this is the true story. The shoe retailers Frank Melville and his son, Ward, teamed up with the shoe manufacturer J. Frank McElwain in 1921 in order to establish a major low-priced shoe store chain. Ward Melville insisted that the name of the chain be identifiably Scandinavian, Scottish, or Irish. He found what he considered to be the perfect name in a golf magazine, but it was too long to fit comfortably and legibly on a shoe label. The partners solved the problem by shortening "Tom McCann" to "Thom McAn," replacing "Thom" for "Tom" in order to give it a more "distinctive" look.

Shoemaking Made Simple
Putting It All Together

The details of shoemaking vary from one style to another. Most quality dress shoes have leather soles, while many casual and athletic shoes have synthetic soles. The processes used to make these synthetic components include vulcanization (used for sneaker soles) and injection molding (for synthetic platforms). Slush molding is a process that turns out an entire one-piece rain boot in a single step. Unconstructed shoes, like moccasins, are stitched together as if they were made of fabric. But most standard shoes are manufactured today using the same ten basic steps that have been used for centuries. Although current technology employs as many as eighty different machines to make a single pair of shoes, custom shoemakers create modern footwear using the same handful of basic tools that were used in ancient Egypt.

Just how do the shoes on your feet start out? The next few pages will give you an overview of the process.

The Parts of the Shoe
Most people can tell the heel from the toe of a shoe, but what about the *details?* How many of the following shoe terms can you define?

1. *Last:* The form, made of wood or plastic, that's used to shape shoes. The last serves as a template, around which leather or fabric is stretched to create an individual shoe. Separate lasts are necessary for each heel height, size, and style of a given shoe. Separate lasts are also required for the right and left feet of a particular shoe style and size. A single last may be used as the foundation for thousands of shoes and may survive many years. In Hong Kong and Europe some shoemakers still custom-make lasts for individual customers, but most of the footwear industry now makes lasts using standardized sizes. The term also refers to the specific shape and size of a shoe, as in "that pump has a pretty last."

THE MAKING-OF-A-SHOE TREE

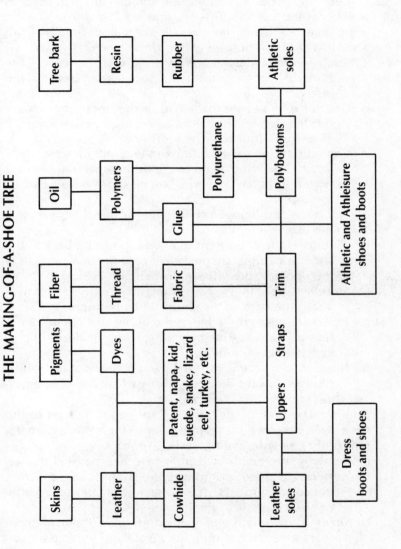

2. *Upper:* The upper is literally the upper part of the shoe, which covers the toes, instep, and back of the foot. The upper may be made from one piece of leather or fabric with a seam at the back or from two or three pieces.
   a. *Vamp* refers to the section of the upper that covers the front of the foot, from the toes as far back as the instep.
   b. *Quarter* refers to the back half of the upper that covers the heel of the foot. It's called a quarter because it covers one fourth of the foot.
   c. *Cap* refers to an extra section of the upper directly covering the toes. It may be of a different material or color than the rest of the shoe. Not all shoes have a cap, or toe cap.
   d. *Puff* refers to a lining in some shoes inside the toe area of the upper.
   e. *Counter* is the equivalent of a toe cap for the back of the shoe. It's a separate piece laid over the heel section of the upper to provide support and/or styling.
   f. *Stiffener* refers to the firm lining inside the heel, which keeps the back of the shoe stiff and upright.
   g. *Topline* refers to the edge of the upper that encircles the foot and ankle. This may be stitched or decorated to give it extra definition.
   h. *Throat* refers to the forward part of the topline, which plunges toward the toes. Throats may be scooped, V-ed, squared, or scalloped.
3. *Bottom:* The bottom includes the sole and the heel of the shoe. Unit bottoms are shaped from a single piece of material (rubber, polyurethane, plastic, wood).
   a. *Insole* is the length of leather or other material that attaches to the upper to give the shoe its shape during the lasting process. The outer sole is later glued and/or sewn directly to the insole.
   b. *Shank* is the length of metal, wood, or synthetic material that's inserted between the insole and outsole following the arch of the foot to provide strength and support.
   c. *Waist* refers to the central section of the shoe, at the point of the arch and instep.

   d. *Feather* refers to the line circling the outside of the shoe where the upper touches the sole.

   e. The *heel* in most shoes is separate from the rest of the sole, though in unit bottoms it is continuous. There are three parts to the heel: the breast, top-piece, and seat. The *breast* is the part of the heel under the arch which faces forward. The *top-piece* is the layer of the heel that strikes the ground. It's often made of plastic or rubber in order to absorb the shock of impact. The top-piece got its name because shoes are held upside down while being made, so this bottom-most piece is seen as the top. The *seat* is the side of the heel that fits onto the sole—in which the shoe "sits."

The Making of a Standard Dress or Casual Shoe

1. *Last making:* The foot-shaped form used to mold and shape the shoe is known as a last. To shape this form, last makers require as many as thirty-five different measurements as fine as a sixty-fourth of an inch. Traditional lasts are carved out of wood, but most manufacturers today make lasts out of polyethylene plastic.

2. *Pattern making:* Measurements taken from the last are used to create patterns for the various upper sections of the shoe. The pattern reflects both the dimensions of the human foot and the specifications of the given shoe design. Leather is cut by hand to match the pattern pieces, then assembled to make up sample shoes, which are shown to prospective buyers. If the number of orders is sizable enough, the shoe proceeds into mass production.

3. *Cutting:* In most factories, the pattern is used to create steel dies that will cut stacks of leather into uniform pieces. Some ultramodern companies have replaced their cutting machines with laser beams, while custom shoemakers still use curved knives to follow patterns.

4. *Fitting:* Cut pieces are stitched together with design details, linings, and lacing sections. Toe boxes and counters that shape and reinforce the heels are inserted into this loosely assembled upper.

5. *Lasting:* The fitted upper is pulled tautly over the last until it looks like a finished shoe. Depending on the complexity of the shape and the quality of the shoe, it will remain on the last anywhere from a few hours to several days.

6. *Stock fitting:* The sole is prepared by layering and gluing together the insole, sock lining, shank, outer sole, and heel.

7. *Bottoming out:* The assembled sole is attached to the upper (still on the last) by one of three methods: cementing, which is used for about 70 percent of shoes made today; molding, which involves slush or injection molding, or vulcanization; or sewing, which is used in the welt or moccasin technique.

8. *Heeling:* The heel may be attached separately using glue and nails. It is then shaved to fit the shoe.

9. *Finishing:* The shoe is polished, then removed from the last. The label is affixed or stamped inside, and heel and toe pads are inserted.

10. *Packing it in:* In the packing room damages are repaired and buckles, bows, and laces are attached. Shoes are boxed and shipped after final cleaning and inspection.

6
FEET FOREVER!

The Stories Behind the Shoes
Shoes Have Ancestors Too

Some shoes were designed for function, some for whimsy, and some purely to satisfy the egos of their creators. Some styles are traceable to a single individual, while others emerged out of collective design efforts. Still others evolved over long periods, with anonymous shoemakers making small adjustments until the style settled into a permanent pattern. The following accounts are some of the more interesting shoe-style histories on record.

Balmorals, or Bals

Queen Victoria's husband, Prince Albert, created this closed throat-laced shoe and named it after the royal residence in Scotland, Balmoral Castle. In the heyday of Queen Victoria, Albert promoted bals as the footwear of choice for fashionable men and women. After arriving in the United States in the late nineteenth century, the balmoral was adapted into ankle-high boots.

THE TREE OF SHOE STYLES
From Mukluks to Mary Janes

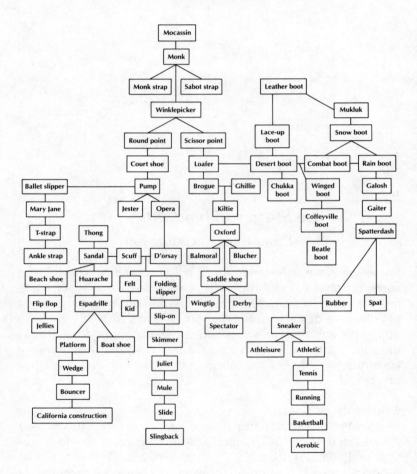

Bluchers

General Gebhard von Blücher was the father of the heavy men's shoe named after him. First designed by the general as an army shoe, the blucher is a lace-up shoe with an open throat and a wide, floppy tongue.

Boots

The earliest boots were actually low-cut shoes or sandals worn with separate protective shin guards or leggings. The standard boot as we know it didn't evolve until about A.D. 1000. Pirates and early merchant navy men were fond of boots because they provided roomy hiding places for smuggled and stolen valuables. This practice became so common among the bandits that it gave rise to the term "bootleg."

Riding Boots

Many of today's fashion boot styles had their beginnings in the hunting boots worn in the British Isles centuries ago, when country squires "rode to the hounds" in order to drive foxes out of their barnyards. The squires wore thigh-high leather boots to protect their legs while riding through rough country. When the hunt was over and the men adjourned to the local pub, they turned down their boot tops in order to bend their knees and relax. Their boots were black with brown linings. Today's women riders wear black boots with black patent cuffs. The fit of riding boots has always been critical. These boots must follow the contour of the leg precisely without the aid of zippers or laces. Custom-made boots cost as much as $700 a pair, and ready-made boots can easily run over $100. The good news is that a quality pair of riding boots may last thirty-five years or more—long enough to be passed on to the next generation of riders. Unfortunately, the same cannot be said of most fashion boots—even those that are stylistic descendants from riding boots.

Cowboy Boots

To the early American cowboy, boots were as important as a ten-gallon hat. He needed this equipment to perform his job and, in fact, thought of his footwear so fondly that he wanted to "die with his boots on," though this distinction generally was reserved for outlaws or lawmen. Then, some time in the late 1960s, the public began to discover the Western boot. Trendsetters were drawn to the nuances of fit, the exotic variety in leathers, and the way these boots could make a macho pose. When the Presidential candidate Ronald Reagan hit the campaign trail in cowboy boots, the word was out. But what really set the Western boot craze on fire was the movie *Urban Cowboy*. When John Travolta Texas-two-stepped his way across the dance floor in *his* cowboy boots, the American public jumped on the trend like a crow on a June bug. The exploding boot market encouraged the adoption of more and more exotic leathers, including but by no means limited to elephant, African tree frog, nocona, antelope, ostrich, sea turtle, kangaroo, anaconda, and even chicken feet and eelskin. Although the boots still roamed where deer and antelope play, they were also seen "uptown" in places like Chicago's Old Town, where they were purchased by the likes of Fleetwood Mac, the Rolling Stones, Led Zeppelin, Emerson, Lake and Palmer, Levar Burton, and members of the Chicago Bears football team. The trend continued until the early 1980s, when fluctuations in the economy forced a decline in luxury purchases. Ritzy shops from Rodeo Drive to Madison Avenue began to mark down their boot stocks for clearance, and those enamored of spaghetti Westerns and urban cowboys cleaned up.

Brogues
The original Irish brogue was made from a single piece of leather gathered around the ankle. When the shoe traveled from Ireland to Scotland, it evolved into the heavier, waterproof brog. With time, the utilitarian features were adjusted for fashion, resulting in today's brogue with perforations and pinking on the toe, vamp, and quarter.

Clogs
The Greeks and Chinese wore them thousands of years ago. In seventeenth-century Venice, chopines lifted women as much as 16 inches above the cobblestones so that the women had to be supported on both sides in order to walk. To this day the

Dutch slip on *klompen* whenever they go outside, and the Scandinavians learn as toddlers how to walk in their *tre sko*. This is more difficult than it may appear according to the Danes, who refer to their clogs as ankle busters.

The first clogs appeared in this country in the form of wooden shoes handcrafted in the late 1930s by Oscar Auestad for University of Oregon coeds. In later years the wooden shoe acquired a leather upper and the wooden soles were exchanged for—or combined with—a variety of materials ranging from rubber to polyurethane. Whether in or out of the fashion spotlight, clogs remained a perennial top seller.

D'orsays

The d'orsay pump was the creation and namesake of Count Alfred Guillaume Gabriel D'Orsay (1801–1852), a leading socialite in French aristocratic circles. His shoe was at first considered a daring departure from the court shoes of the era. Its revealing plunge at the instep created a highly unorthodox silhouette for the shoe and reshaped the exposed foot. In a short time, however, the shoe became the rage of the continent, and one-sided and two-sided d'orsays remain popular today.

Huaraches

The huarache is a traditional shoe in Mexico. Originally woven out of thick tan leather straps, the term now applies to similar-looking sandals made out of synthetics, fabrics, plastics, or dyed leathers as well. The shoe wasn't imported to the United States until 1927, when the Old Mexico Shop in Santa Fe, New Mexico, became the first American retailer to sell the shoe. The huarache arrived in Miami Beach resorts in 1934, along with other open-toed sandals, and received its first national advertising in 1936. Ultimately, the sandals became so popular that U.S. factories began importing Mexican laborers to weave the footwear on this side of the border.

Jellies

Plastic and rubber shoes came into existence with the initial development of plastic. Popular at the beach or pool, the earliest version of these shoes were called thongs or flip-flops.

In the 1980s, as the athletic-shoe business dipped, many factories that had made the synthetic-soled footwear in the Orient were forced to close down. In Japan these factories looked for new applications for their vulcanization equipment. Jellies were the answer. These shoes were injection-molded or vulcanized, sandalized, and fashionable. The craze caught on from the city streets of Brazil to the beaches of California. Designers joined in, and for a few seasons shoe stores throughout the world were filled with this colorful, inexpensive footwear.

Kilties
The shoe with the slashed "shawl tongue" over the lacing was first worn by women athletes in Greece as early as 100 B.C. It came into favor again among European peasants, but it wasn't until the prince of Wales took a shine to it in the 1920s that the kiltie made its leap into the modern fashion world.

Mocassins
Mocassins vie with sandals for the position of oldest shoe type. The first mocassin was probably a piece of hide, leaves, or woven grasses wrapped and tied around the foot. The most familiar version of the mocassin in this country was created by native Americans. Each tribe had its own distinctive style so that it was possible to identify an Indian's tribal affiliation by checking his footwear. The designs, made with natural materials like porcupine quills and shells, were based on religious beliefs. The colonists adopted the mocassin largely because of economic circumstances. Shoemakers were few and far between in colonial America, and standard European-style shoes had to be custom-made. The cost was beyond the means of most colonists, so they learned from the native Americans to stitch up mocassins themselves. The shoes became so popular in America that they eventually were exported to England. They became so popular in England that local shoemakers, feeling threatened, pushed through laws prohibiting further importation of mocassins to England from the Colonies.

Monks

These familiar cross-strapped slip-ons date back to European monasteries of about A.D. 1400. The first version of this shoe was designed by an Alpine monk. Eventually, it spun off a clog version and at least one style of loafer.

Mules

The first mules were devised during the Elizabethan period to slip over dress shoes to protect them from the filth of the streets. They were then called pattens. Also known as slides, these slip-on shoes have neither sides nor back. They consist simply of a high slidelike vamp with a closed toe or strap across the instep. Through the years these "vampish" sandals have won favor with streetwalkers, college coeds, and housewives, though rarely all at once. In the 1960s an elastic band was added under the inner sole, and the shoes were dubbed springalators (a twist on the shoe term "elevators").

Oxfords for Men

Lace-up oxfords, appropriately, made their worldwide debut in the late 1800s at Oxford University in England. The shoes, inspired by women's lace-up corsets, were favorites among the university students. The first men's oxfords in the United States were made of light tan calfskin and retailed for $2.50 a pair. The year was 1898, the place was Binghamton, New York. The shoes were on sale, but the store owner, a Mr. Skinner, was not pleased. He cornered the supplier of the shoes and demanded that boot tops be put on the oxfords so that they would sell faster.

Oxfords for Women

Oxfords made their way into the wardrobes of women by the early 1920s. Although they were considered bulky if not down-right ugly, these shoes eventually became a fad, thanks to First Lady Eleanor Roosevelt. For Eleanor, the shoe represented the priority of comfort over style. For the rest of American women, it represented a way to keep pace with the folks in the White House.

Pumps

The original pump was a woman's low-cut slipper of the mid-sixteenth century, but the shoe was not named until the nineteenth century. The name came from male carriage drivers who wore the low-heeled slippers because they eased the job of pumping the hydraulic mechanisms of the carriages of the day.

Sandals

The first footwear of the warmer climates in ancient times, sandals have been found in Egyptian burials dating back to 7000 B.C. and even earlier. The earliest sandals were made from papyrus and reeds, but the shoe got its name from the Romans, who called it *sanis,* a thong attached to a board of leather.

Wellingtons

Arthur Wellesley, the first duke of Wellington and the British commander who defeated Napoleon at Waterloo in 1815, first popularized this boot. The original Wellington had a low, flat heel and a square toe that sometimes had a red piece of leather sewn over the top. The boots stretched to the knee and were cut lower at the back of the leg than in the front, to allow free knee movement.

Shoes for Everyone and Every Feat

From Tiny Tots to Astronauts

Many of us were given our first pair of baby booties before we were born—and we're likely to be wearing our last pair of shoes even after we die. Between the two extremes in life, we go through as many changes in footwear as we do in physical size, temperament, ambition, and fashion orientation. The shoe industry somehow manages to keep in step with our personal changes by providing designs to satisfy every customer at every age.

When you get right down to it, a shoe is supposed to be functional. Whether the function is walking or loafing, river rafting or tree climbing, the purpose of shoes is to help you perform efficiently, comfortably, and safely. That sounds like a fairly boring challenge, but once you get past the ho-hum selection of duty shoes and sensible shoes, you may find some functional creations that surprise you. There are literally shoes for every purpose—and the more intriguing the purpose the more amusing the shoe is likely to be.

Today there is specialized footwear for every activity. Much of it is designed and manufactured by the sports aficionados themselves. White water river guide Mark Thatcher, for example, designed a sandal with an ankle grip specifically for rafting wear. Japanese fishermen were the first to design a special sock-and-rubber bootie that protects feet walking on rocky shorelines. These are now manufactured in this country for use by rafters and river fishermen.

Expert mountaineers routinely advise manufacturers and test new versions of hiking, mountain climbing, and ice climbing footwear that may cost as much as $300 per pair. Because cold weather sports are becoming increasingly popular among the wealthy, and because the price tags on this footwear are high, there is fierce competition among manufacturers to capture the market. Consequently, mountaineering and ski boots are among the most hi-tech products in the industry.

As the variety of sports fads increases, the footwear industry scrambles to keep up with the trends. There are now shoes designed specifically for sports such as aerobic dancing, board sailing, kayaking, parachuting, skateboarding, and triathloning, as well as the sport of walking. Wherever the pacesetters may be, "featwear" manufacturers are never far behind!

International Footwear Parade
Global Fashions Below the Belt

Western shoes and fashions have always been subject to fre-
quent—often whimsical or downright silly—design trends. Not
so the traditional folk costumes of the less faddish nations of
the world. In these countries national costumes are preserved
over centuries in honor of the cultural past. Ironically, the
trendy modern-day designers also benefit from the preserva-
tion of traditional "footnotes"; many of these designs recur in
the displays of shops on Madison Avenue and Rodeo Drive.
Just take note of the shoes in your closet that match the footwear fashions listed below.

GEOGRAPHIC REGION	FOOTWEAR STYLES
Afghanistan	No Afghani costume is complete without a pair of peak-toed slippers made of soft, dyed leather. These slippers are borrowed from the Turkish slippers of Ali Baba fame.
Tropical Africa	The heat of tropical Africa makes shoes of any weight uncomfortable. As a result, the traditional footgear of most African nations is a minimal sandal or, better yet, ankle jewelry worn with *no* soled footwear.
Albania	Like the Afghani, the Albanians borrowed the turned-up, peak-toed slippers of their Turkish neighbors.
Algeria	This North African country has combined the best of its northern and southern neighbors. Like the Islamic countries bordering the Mediterranean, Algeria has adopted soft slippers as one form of traditional footwear. The slippers are

GEOGRAPHIC REGION   FOOTWEAR STYLES

of rose-colored suede. The hitch is that they're worn with gold anklets like those worn in African cultures farther south. Some Algerians trend even more in the direction of southern Africa by foregoing the slippers entirely and stenciling or tattooing their feet with henna.

Argentina

In the home of the South American cowboy, the natural footgear are boots made of thick black leather.

Armenia

The idea of wearing bobby socks may have come first from Armenia, where the traditional shoe is a soft boot made of red moroccan leather and worn with white socks.

Austria

In Austria the T-strap has been around for years. The national shoe for women is a black flat with a T-strap buckle.

Brazil

Remember the metallics (shoes with the gleaming finish of silver, gold, or bronze) of a few years back? Brazil had them first. The national Brazilian shoe is a pointy-toed slipper made of bronze leather and tied with ribbons.

Burma

Color is the keynote in the cultural footwear of Burma. The shoes are flat Chinese-style slippers, but they must be red.

Cambodia

There's not much to the Cambodian shoe in terms of construction, but look at the detail! They're flat backless slippers with a closed toe

GEOGRAPHIC REGION   FOOTWEAR STYLES

encrusted with gold and silver
embroidery and jewels.

Canada

Function dictates form in Canada,
where the national footwear is a fur
boot with rubber soles.

China

For outside wear, the Chinese
traditionally wore wooden clog-type
shoes with leather thongs. When
inside, the clogs were traded for
delicate slippers of silk or cotton.
The lotus shoe created for bound
feet was the national ladies' shoe for
more than a century, but it became a
relic when footbinding was
outlawed in China in 1911.

Czechoslovakia

The Czechs may win the prize for
the sexiest national footwear on this
list. The shoes are black—either silk
slippers or high-laced leather
shoes—and they're worn with bright
red stockings.

Denmark

The traditional Danish costume
includes white-leather boots lined
with fur. They're trimmed with lace
and embroidery and worn over bare
feet.

Finland

The Finnish national shoe is called a
carbatine. It's fashioned out of tree
bark or undressed leather and
bound with colored cloth ties.

Greece

Greece offers a choice of two
traditional shoes. One is a black
leather slipper with red or blue
pompoms on the toes. The other is
a peak-toed shoe called *itsaruchia*.

GEOGRAPHIC REGION	FOOTWEAR STYLES

India

True to its division of major religions, India has two basic styles of national footgear. Reflecting the Islamic influence are the soft dyed leather peak-toed slippers worn with brown leggings. Traditional Hindu costumes call for bejeweled leather sandals.

Japan

The Japanese platform thongs, or *geta,* have a wooden sole raised on two parallel crossbars. They are usually worn with *tabi,* the cotton ankle-high socks that have a mittenlike shape so that they fit around the *geta*'s velvet thongs. Peasants traditionally wear straw thong sandals called *zori* with *tabi.*

Korea

Korea's delicate national shoes are certainly *not* made for walking beyond ritual ceremonies. These boots are made of black felt and velvet, piped with white trim.

Mongolia

When it arrived on American fashion pages in the 1960s, we called it the Cossack look, but it may have originated in Mongolia. Full trousers are worn tucked into the tops of tall black boots.

Netherlands

The customary Dutch footwear is actually a combination pack: wooden clogs, or pattens, for wearing outside, and dark blue knitted hose with leather feet for wearing shoe-free indoors.

GEOGRAPHIC REGION	FOOTWEAR STYLES
Philippines	The Filipino favorite is a shoe that takes the form of a clog but is called a *sapatilla*. It's made of any available material, including cloth, straw, wood, or imported leather.
Poland	The most colorful of the Polish costumes call for soft black leather shoes, called *bottines*, laced with a blue ribbon and worn over pink stockings.
Russia	The traditional Russian costume includes red or black leather boots with white cuffs striped in red and black leather and fringed with red tassels. They reach to mid thigh and may be ornately decorated. Throughout the USSR peasants and workers ordinarily wear tall black boots that rise to the knee, at which point the pant legs buckle over them.
Saudi Arabia	Another country that believes in barefoot color is Saudi Arabia. Women's feet are dyed brown to match their face veils—and to toughen their feet for walking without shoes.
Scotland	Spats may be out of fashion in America, but they're still part of the cultural costume of Scotland. They're worn buttoned over black shoes with tartan socks.
Spain	The original Broadway dance shoe was worn by gypsy flamenco

GEOGRAPHIC REGION   FOOTWEAR STYLES

dancers. The customary black shoe has a short shapely heel, rounded toe, and a strap that buttons across the instep.

Thailand

Old-fashioned Siamese footwear is shaped like a canoe with an open toe. The sole is of wood, and the upper, of wood and cloth embroidered with gold and silver thread.

Tibet

Surprisingly, the traditional boot of Tibet is made not of leather but of felt. Warmth and sturdiness are provided by the boot's fur lining.

Turkey

The traditional Turkish slipper is called a *babouche*. It has the characteristic upturned and pointed toe. These soft leather shoes are dyed in bright colors—red, yellow, or blue. They may also be made of red velvet.

Uruguay

One early version of the now familiar espadrille is the *alpargatas*, the national shoe of Uruguay. Like espadrilles elsewhere in South America and Spain, these slip-on shoes are made of canvas with coiled-rope soles.

Footwear Trade Fairs Year Round
For a Glimpse of Footwear Futures

If you have an avid interest in footwear, you'll want to know about the major trade shows where next year's shoe fashions make their debut. Small regional shows are held throughout the year, but most manufacturers hold their most exciting designs for the large international shows, which vary in importance from year to year. Shows are open to the trade only, but shoe aficionados can dream.

JANUARY: Couromoda, Sao Paulo, Brazil
FEBRUARY: National Shoe Fair/FFANY, New York
MARCH: Micam/Modacalzatura, Milan, Italy
    Footwear Fashions, Dusseldorf, Germany
MAY: Lineanelle, Bologna, Italy
JUNE: Modatecc, Elda, Spain
AUGUST: National Shoe Fair/FFANY, New York
SEPTEMBER: Micam, Bologna, Italy
    Footwear Fashions, Dusseldorf, Germany
NOVEMBER: Modatecc, Elda, Spain

7

BOTTOM LINE TRIVIA

How to Tell If the Shoe Fits

A Shoe Store Survival Guide

There's more to shoes than meets the feet, but the way in which a shoe *does* meet your foot may well determine how long it stays on your foot. In order to understand the nuances of shoe sizing and fit, it may help to first explore the way your feet are built and how they work.

The foot is constructed like an elongated hand with a great deal of extra padding to absorb impact. Technically, the foot starts with the seven cubelike bones that comprise the ankle, or tarsus. The ankle is equivalent to the wrist on the hand, serving as a hinge that moves the foot backward and forward. The largest bone in the ankle, which we usually call the heel, is the calcaneus. This one bone receives the full shock of every step we take.

In many animals the calcaneus has moved up the leg in the course of evolution. In horses and dogs it no longer touches the ground at all, and the animals, in effect, are walking on their toes. Scientists warn that another 5,000 years of high-heeled fashions may set chic women on the same evolutionary course. Even within a single woman's lifetime constant wearing of high heels can cause a permanent shortening of the calf muscles. Women who have this condition cannot walk bare-foot or in flat shoes without considerable difficulty and pain.

The ankle leads to the metatarsus, Greek for "in front of the tarsus." The five long metatarsal bones are wrapped in a paral-lel configuration by a bundle of strong fibrous tissues. These tissues protect the foot and also support its two arches, one lengthwise and the other across the foot. These arches are responsible for spring and flexibility in movement. Movement of the metatarsus and the tarsus is controlled by the leg mus-cles.

Extending from the metatarsals are the fourteen phalanges, the bones that make up our toes. The function of the pha-langes is to help us balance. The big toes each consist of two bones. Each of the others consists of three and is moved by specific muscles in the feet. Nine of the nineteen foot muscles are reserved for movement of the big toe alone.

The most important padding in the foot is the layer of fibrous tissue called the plantar fascia, which runs the length of the sole, from the toes down the length of the foot and around to the back of the heel.

How the Foot Works

The foot is arranged around three weight-bearing points: the heel, the base of the little toe, and the base of the big toe. Each of these points comes into play with every step we take. First the foot impacts on the heel. Next it rolls forward moving the stress to the base of the little toe. Finally the roll is completed at the base of the big toe, and the toe pushes off into the next step.

The biomechanics of walking, of course, differ from other athletic activities, such as ballet, basketball, bicycling, and skat-ing. These activities alter the formula of movement set for walking and place more stress on some points and less on others. Cyclists, for example, exert a great deal of force on the cross-section of the foot from the big toe to the little toe. They don't impact on the heel at all. Ballerinas on pointe place the most pressure on the phalanges themselves, and their feet generally show the painful signs of this unnatural wear and tear. Because these activities do vary the function of the foot so greatly, it's essential to have the proper footwear to minimize shock and damage.

The Shoes Make the Feet

For the best fit and maximum comfort, keep the following tips in mind the next time you shop for shoes:

1. Buy your shoes in early afternoon, after you've been standing or walking for a few hours and your feet have had a chance to swell. The idea is to measure your feet when they're at their maximum size, because it's much better to have a shoe slightly too large than too small.

2. Have your feet measured each time you buy new shoes. Even adult feet change size with age and changes in weight. Have both feet measured, because there's often a difference in size between the two. Buy for the larger foot. You can always use shoe pads to improve the fit on the smaller shoe. Stand up while your feet are being measured in order to register any change in dimension your shoes will have to absorb as you stand or walk.

3. Try on both shoes, and walk around the store. Check for gapping at the sides, slippage at the heel, and tightness over the instep. If any of these checkpoints are less than perfect, don't buy the shoes.

4. Make sure you have between ¼ and ½ inch of space in each shoe between your longest toe, which may not be your big toe, and the tip of the shoe. There shouldn't be any pressure on the tops of your toes. If you don't have the room, look for another pair of shoes.

5. Make sure the parts of your feet fit comfortably into the corresponding parts of the shoe. Foot to shoe, the following proportions should match: distance of the heel to ball of the foot; height of the foot-shoe at the ball of the foot; curvature and height of the heel.

6. Don't get cute about sizes ("Oh, my feet are so petite. Of *course* I wear a 6," when you know very well you wear a

7½). Shoe sizes vary widely from manufacturer to manufacturer, so a 6 from one company may well be a 7½ from another. Only your feet will know for sure, and *you'll* pay the price if you try to fool them.

7. Don't count on shoes "breaking in" to become more comfortable. If they're not comfortable in the store, there's a good chance they'll never be comfortable. This is especially true of shoes made from synthetic materials, which always return to their original shape no matter how hard you may try to stretch them.
8. Check the construction of the shoes. Seams should be straight, linings smooth and without gaps. The insole should extend all the way to meet the upper on all sides.
9. Wear socks or stockings the same thickness you expect to wear with the shoes.
10. Remember that the smaller the strike area (the part of the foot that hits the ground) in the sole, the more weight is concentrated on that spot. High heels narrow the strike area and heighten the strain on legs and feet. Reserve these shoes for sitting-down wear, not walking and standing.

Special Tips for Fitting Boots

1. If you have a high instep, make sure your boots have zippers. Otherwise, you may have trouble getting the boots on and off.
2. If the boot has a zipper that opens all the way down, make sure it curves toward the toe at the bottom.
3. Never buy boots that are too loose. Slipping and sliding in boots almost always results in blisters, sores, calluses, and a host of other foot complaints.
4. Be alert to the unique fits of certain boot styles. Western boots are designed to slip slightly at the heel when first purchased; that will lessen as the footwear breaks in and begins to mold itself to the shape of the foot. Boots with flat heels need to be slightly larger than boots with high heels, since the feet tend to spread in flat footwear.
5. Take your figure and weight into consideration when buying boots. If you have heavy legs, wear straight, stand-up boots with loose tops that don't press on the flesh or cut circulation. Leave the squashy, clingy boots for thin legs.

The Perfect Fit

Is there a perfect shoe size? According to old-school Chinese custom, a woman's feet had to be bound and the woman effectively crippled in order to attain the ideal shoe size. Today's shoe industry doesn't require physical disfigurement, but it does prefer small sizes over all others. For women the ideal size is 6, for men it's size 8½. These are sample sizes, and the whole footwear industry, in a sense, revolves around them.

Nearly every shoe style is first constructed in sample size. Salesmen then travel with these diminutive samples in order to show them to prospective buyers at department and shoe stores around the world. At trade conventions manufacturers hire models with tiny feet to demonstrate the shoes for retailers, who then place orders for the full range of sizes.

There are two major reasons why these small sizes are selected for samples. First, most shoes look best in tiny sizes. (While Americans are more relaxed on the subject than the traditional Chinese, they too accept the conventional attitude that little feet are more appealing than large ones, especially when it comes to women's feet.) Part of the challenge for retailers is to tell by looking at a sample size whether a particular style will also be attractive in larger sizes, which constitute most of the consumer purchases in America.

The second reason for small sample sizes is economic. The smaller the shoe, the less leather, fabric, time, and money it will take to make. When you consider that a majority of the thousands of shoe styles released each season never get past the sample stage, it makes sense to keep their cost to a bare minimum. The smaller sizes also weigh less and fit more easily into sample cases, easing the load of shoe salesmen, who frequently carry a hundred or more shoes at a time.

What happens to the thousands of pairs of samples after retailers have placed their orders? Some are sold through sample outlets. Some are given away to shoe models, and some are simply dumped. If you're lucky enough to wear a sample size, you can save a fortune on new shoes just by shopping in the right places at the right times of the year.

The Truth About Shoe Salesmen
If you're considering a new career, you might be interested to learn that the salaries of top shoe sales representatives can be well into the six figures. Condescending jokes about shoe salesmen aside, many of those who are in this business swear by it. But what some consider to be benefits, others might view as drawbacks. For an overview of life in shoe sales, take a look at the results of a survey conducted in 1979 by the shoe sales representatives' professional organization, the National Shoe Traveler's Association.

- The typical American shoe rep is between the ages of forty and forty-nine, married, with children.
- The typical American shoe rep is male, though women reps are on the increase.
- The typical American shoe rep works solely on commission.
- In a year, the typical American shoe sales rep averages
—255 days on the road
—159 nights in hotels in a 3½-state territory
—more than 85 calls on retail outlets in a sales trip
—expenses of almost $30,000, which in the vast majority of cases are paid by the reps themselves
—a substantial increase in commissions and earnings over the past year

Shoe industry executives also fare well, as can be seen from the table.

TEN HIGHEST PAID SHOE INDUSTRY EXECUTIVES OF 1981*

EXECUTIVE AND TITLE	COMPANY	TOTAL COMPEN-SATION
Lionel Levy, chairman and CEO	Felsway, Inc.	$1,468,728
Stuart Weitzman, vice-president	Caressa, Inc.	$ 964,469
George Kaye, president	Felsway Corp.	$ 828,409
Kenneth E. Berland, president	Melville Corp.	$ 732,572

EXECUTIVE AND TITLE	COMPANY	TOTAL COMPEN- SATION
Herbert Schiff, chairman, president, and CEO	Scoa, Inc.	$ 717,371
Francis C. Rooney, Jr., Chairman and CEO	Melville Corp.	$ 662,597
Philip G. Barach, chairman, president and CEO	U.S. Shoe Corp.	$ 451,250
W. L. Hadley Griffin, chairman	Brown Group, Inc.	$ 416,384
John Hanigan, chairman and CEO	Genesco, Inc.	$ 415,710
B. A. Bridgewater, Jr., president and CEO	Brown Group, Inc.	$ 405,636

SOURCE: *Footwear News Magazine,* 1982.
*Average executive compensation was $305,217, approximately 31 percent less than the bonus and salary averages of CEOs in other industries surveyed by *Forbes* magazine in 1982.

Special Tips for Fitting Children

1. You can count on children's feet to grow wildly just after you've invested in a new imported—and *expensive*—pair of party shoes. To ward off heartache and pocketbook strain, keep the following growth timetable in mind:

Age	*Check Shoe Size*
2–6	Every 1–2 months
6–10	Every 2–3 months
10–12	Every 3–4 months
12–15	Every 4–5 months
15–20	Every 6 months

2. Never try to cut financial corners by resorting to hand-me-down shoes. You'll pay the price—and more—in your child's foot problems later on. Shoes generally conform to the feet

of the wearer, and since no two feet are exactly alike, it's doubtful that your first child's shoes will be comfortable for your second child.

3. Young children will rarely speak up when they're in discomfort. Either they can't pinpoint the cause of their distress, or they're too busy playing to pay attention. Also, since their feet are not fully formed, too small shoes may feel fine to them. It's up to you to learn the unspoken signs of improper shoe fit:

   a. *If your child keeps taking off his or her shoes, they may be too small.*

   b. *If your child is limping, the shoes may be the cause.*

   c. *Look for tears or pulls in the lining of the shoes. These are signs that the shoes are pressing too hard in the wrong places.*

   d. *Examine your child's feet soon after taking off shoes. If there are red marks across the tops of the toes or on the sides of the feet, the shoes are probably too tight.*

   e. *Check the soles for signs of uneven wear. If the soles or heels are considerably more worn on one side than the other, your child may have foot or ankle problems. Check with a podiatrist to see if shoe inserts or corrective shoes are in order.*

   f. *Have your child's feet measured at regular intervals.*

What to Look for in Athletic Shoes

Shopping for Shoes on the Move

The running boom that began in the 1970s is still going strong, and as a result, there are hundreds of shoes to fit the fad. Individual pairs can range anywhere from $15 to $150 or more for custom-made shoes. To make matters even more confusing, the athletic shoe manufacturers are introducing new models constantly, so if you've finally found the "perfect" shoe for your foot, you may be out of luck when you try to buy a second pair six months from now.

The perpetual turnover in running shoes does reflect some very real advances in athletic footwear technology, however. According to *Running Times* magazine, there are five major trends in running-shoe design today:

1. Manufacturers are gearing their design process to meet the very different needs of two basic types of runners—those who require stability and control and those who desire cushioning foremost. Within these categories are countless subgroups, but these two sets of criteria are primary to the design of today's running shoe.

2. The industry is now designing shoes for the full range of running appetites. Previously, manufacturers assumed that a shoe that pleased a marathoner or track star would automatically win over the weekend athletes. Now shoe companies are designing shoes that are lighter, more streamlined, and suited for the occasional jogger rather than the elite athlete.

3. Increasingly, the trend in athletic shoe design is toward balance. By closely examining the motion and impact levels at all parts of the running foot, technicians can fine-tune the cushioning and support in corresponding parts of the shoe. For example, the soles of running shoes may have different densities at various points between heel and toe. They may have deep cushioning in one spot and rigid support in another.

4. Manufacturers are beginning to pay more attention to durability. Some of the materials previously used in running shoes would flatten or deteriorate with time and wear. Because of the way they were constructed, the shoes would quickly lose their shape. Now footwear companies are developing materials that wear longer and new construction techniques to maintain the form of a shoe over months, if not years.

5. The chemistry of the midsole section of running shoes has been a thorn in the side of manufacturers for some time. At present, most midsoles are made of a material called EVA (Ethyl Vinyl Acetate). The positive aspect of this material is that it is very light and yet offers good cushioning. The drawbacks are that it gradually compresses, losing its cushioning power and throwing the strike of the foot off

balance. Major athletic shoe companies are now experimenting with alternatives to EVA. Nike, for example, has recently introduced a midsole material called Phylon, which the company claims "provides 35% better cushioning and resiliency than the best conventional EVA." Polyurethane may be the key to the ultimate EVA alternative. It's heavy and stiff, but when combined with lighter materials, it runs a close equal to EVA without the buckling effect. Industry insiders predict that a new trend in midsole construction will be established in the next couple of years.*

The Features that Make a Running Shoe Run

When buying a shoe for running, ask yourself how you want your shoe to "behave," then check to see if the shoe has the features that will enable it to meet your needs.

For Motion Control

The following features of the shoe stabilize the foot when it comes down or steps off and counteract any imbalances in the runner's movement that might cause injury.

1. *Heel counter:* the semirigid heel cup that prevents your heel from slipping or moving sideways. The counter should be made of tough materials that won't crumple from wetness or wear.
2. *Heel-counter support collar:* A plastic strip that interfaces the counter and the sole to provide additional protection against slipping or rolling of the heel.
3. *Trampoline outsole:* A design pattern of the sole that provides a horseshoe shape of tread at the heel to maximize stability.
4. *Wear-resistant outsole:* A sole made of highly durable material that does not wear down easily. This guards against imbalance caused by compression or abrasion.
5. *Dual-density midsole:* A method of layering materials in the sole so that one layer provides cushioning while the next offers stability and support.

*Running Times, October 1984.

6. *Motion control pillar:* A plug of extremely dense and durable material that is inserted into the sole toward the outside of the heel. This plug lends added resistance to the motion called pronation, the rolling of the foot toward the instep upon heel strike. This rolling motion can cause serious knee injuries.
7. *Forefoot stabilizer strap:* A band of material, usually leather, that wraps around the instep to center the foot during step-off.
8. *Board-last construction:* A style of shoe construction that uses a firm insole, or "board," as the platform of the shoe. Board-lasted shoes are more rigid and less flexible than slip-lasted shoes, which are made without a central insole.

For Cushioning and Comfort

1. *Shaped bottom:* The bottom surface of the sole is constructed as a modified concave shape by building up the surface along the edge of the foot. As the foot comes down, it gently bounces from the center of the sole. This trampoline effect provides the sensation and comfort of extra cushioning without extra materials or weight in the shoe.
2. *Blown rubber sole:* Blown rubber is rubber that, in effect, has been pumped full of air to make it light and springy. It is sometimes used to provide maximum cushioning in a shoe. The drawback is that this material wears out more quickly than solid rubber.
3. *Soft midsole:* EVA is the standard cushioning now used in running-shoe midsoles. Some shoes designed to be worn by ultralight runners and sprinters have only EVA in the midsoles, but shoes for more typical runners have combined midsoles, which are more durable and hold their shape longer than pure EVA.
4. *Metatarsal pad:* Padding may be inserted toward the forefoot of the sole to provide extra softness during push-off.
5. *Achilles tendon notch:* Some shoe models have a notch at the top of the heel counter to prevent rubbing against the Achilles tendon.

For Lightness and Flexibility

1. *Slip-last construction:* Slip lasting, as opposed to board lasting, means that a shoe is made without a board in the sole to
   provide firmness and shape. Generally speaking, slip-lasted
   shoes are lighter and more flexible than board-lasted shoes.
2. *Midsole channels:* Some lightweight models have slices cut
   into or through the midsole to provide greater flexibility of
   movement.
3. *Pig suede upper:* Pig suede is lighter and stronger than other
   leathers used in athletic shoes. In lightweight models it is
   often combined with nylon mesh to minimize weight.

For Durability

1. *Abrasion-resistant outsole:* To protect against the constant
   rubbing of the sole against pavement, many shoes have
   soles with a layer of solid polyurethane or carbon rubber
   along the bottom. For maximum durability and protection,
   make sure this bottom layer is relatively thick, especially at
   the point of heel strike (left corner, left foot; right corner,
   right foot), which in most runners absorbs the greatest
   amount of shock.
2. *High-density midsole:* The most durable shoes will have far
   less EVA in the midsoles than lightweight shoes. Soft materials are strategically used in parts of the sole that require
   maximum cushioning, denser materials in areas that need
   the most protection against compression.

Tracking Down the Best Running Shoe for You

The Perfect Fit
Don't shop for running shoes the way you shop for street
shoes. After you've determined which features in a shoe are
important for your pace, weight, and style of running, survey
the available running-shoe models for three or four candidates.
When you try them on, don't make excuses for them if they
don't immediately feel comfortable. Athletic shoes should not
need breaking in. They should give you plenty of breathing
room around the toes but fit snugly at the heel.

Several companies now make shoes with optical lacing patterns to accommodate variations in foot widths. These offer one alternative for people with wide or narrow feet. Some manufacturers also cater to the hard-to-fit or those who pronate. New Balance offers widths ranging from B through EEEE for men, from AA through D for women. Vans's sizes range from AAAA through EEEEE. With these choices, there's no reason to settle for a less-than-perfect fit.

The Perfect Price Tag

On the one hand, prices are going up. The increasing number of upscale runners have created a market for "elite" running shoes, and manufacturers have responded with enthusiasm. New Balance, Nike, and Saucony are just a few of the companies that offer shoes with price tags of $100 or more. Custom-made shoes from outfits like Bart Hersey's Hersey Custom Shoe Company may exceed $160, but then they *are* made for your feet, and your feet alone.

On the other hand, the running boom has spread to the middle and lower echelons as well, creating an even larger demand for midpriced running shoes. Competition among the numerous athletic shoe manufacturers and high turnover in shoe models have also conspired to keep midlevel prices down. If you're a dedicated runner, you still may need to pay $50 for a shoe that will meet your needs, but chances are you'll get far more kick for the price today than you did a year ago.

What to Look for in Cycling Shoes

Cycling is a sports craze that's been sidling up alongside of running for the last few years. According to surveys by the Bata Shoe Company, one of the major manufacturers of cycling footgear, the typical adult cyclist is between twenty-one and thirty-nine years of age, holds a college degree, and has an annual income of over $30,000. These enthusiasts don't stop with the bicycle. They buy the helmets, the gloves, the clothing, the water bottles—and, of course, the shoes.

The shoe market caters to three distinct types of cyclists, each of which requires a distinctly different type of shoe. These three categories are recreational cyclists (or tourers), competitive racing cyclists, and BMX riders. These last, most of whom are between the ages of five and twenty-five, are adherents of motorcross, the latest cycling craze.

Recreational cyclists use bikes as leisure vehicles. They ride for fun and for exercise, and they combine riding with walking, hiking, or sightseeing. For this reason, they need a shoe that has the stiffness to remain comfortable on the pedal and also the flexibility to function as a walking shoe. To achieve this marriage, most touring shoes have a stiff inner shank of plastic or metal plus nonslip but walkable soles made of polyurethane or rubber.

Racing cyclists are intent only on riding as fast as they can. They want a shoe with maximum function on the bike. It must remain firmly on the pedal. It must be stiff to provide maximum leverage and foot support. It must be lightweight. To fully meet the status standards of diehard racers, it probably must be black in color and imported from either France or Italy, where this sport is far more widely appreciated.

The traditional European models have wooden inner soles lined with leather outsoles. Many newer models have replaced the wood with plastic, steel or nylon. To hold the foot to the pedal, they have cleats under the forefoot. Uppers are usually made of perforated leather or nylon mesh, which breathes without stretching or losing shape.

BMX riders—or dirt racers—need protection and durability as they ride and jump over steeply banked motorcross courses. These riders use their feet off the pedal almost as much as on. They need traction and ankle support. Because of the faddish nature of the sport, the look of the shoe is almost more important than function. Ideally, the shoe should look like a cross between a combat boot and a racquetball shoe, with logos and labels galore.

Although some of the larger athletic shoe companies produce a few cycling shoe styles, this market is dominated by a few of its own majors. For racing and touring models, the leaders are: Bata (the first to come out with a touring shoe in the United States), Sidi of Italy, Detto Pietro of Italy, Le Coq Sportif of France, Marresi of Italy, Duegi of Italy, and Avocet of France.

For BMX shoes, the front-runners are all American: Keds, Vans, and Bata.

Keeping in Step

A Point-by-Point Guide to Footwear Maintenance

Many people assume that a quick polish every couple of months is all that's required to keep a pair of expensive shoes in their prime. The connoisseur knows that quality shoe care requires as much love and attention as the conservation of fine works of art. Shoes require grooming and protection from the moment you bring them home, if you truly want to preserve them longer than a single season. For optimal results, observe the following tips.

Step One: Prime Your New Boots and Shoes

1. Sand down the soles of new footwear to prevent slipping.
2. Use silicone spray on the insides of new boots to help glide them on and off more easily. Silicone also makes footwear water-resistant and helps reduce foot odor.
3. Rub down new suede shoes with a terrycloth towel to remove loose bits of the nap. Then spray with a suede stain guard.
4. Make outdoor shoes water-resistant by spraying them with silicone or applying mink oil. Spray silicone only around the sole and seams. For suede, use waterproofing products made for suede; do not use mink oil.

Step Two: Maintain Your Shoes

1. Polish footwear regularly to guard against scuffing and water damage. To maximize shine and finish, wipe footwear clean after each wearing.
2. Keep the soles and heels of your shoes in good repair. Never let heels wear down past the lifts. Mend broken stitching while the damage is minimal.
3. Keep a pair or two of spare shoes for walking in the rain.
4. When storing footwear for extended periods of time, use shoe and boot trees to keep them in shape. Wooden shoe trees are superior to plastic ones because they absorb moisture.

5. Keep shoes away from heat sources. Leather dries out and becomes misshapen when exposed to heat.
6. Dip the ends of shoelaces in glue to keep them from fraying.
7. Pay special attention to suede. Rub after each wearing with an art gum eraser to prevent buildup of dirt. Use a metal suede brush on dark spots, and if that doesn't work, use the smooth side of an emery board.

Step Three: Polish Properly

1. Wipe shoes clean before you apply any polish.
2. Use circular strokes to work polish into the leather, and use a soft applicator, such as a powder puff or cotton balls.
3. Look for enriched polishes with color to cover up scuffed spots. For major scuffs on white shoes, touch up the damaged spots with white typewriter correction fluid, then polish.
4. Select shoe polishes with care. Look for products that clean, condition, and polish. Avoid liquid polishes, which contain alcohol and will dry out leather if used frequently. If you must use them, alternate with a rich cream polish. For delicate leathers, use a lighter cream or oil product. Never use petroleum jelly on patent leather, as it can damage synthetic patents. Instead, use products specifically made to clean and polish patents.
5. Use saddle soap for cleaning thick leather, but wash it off while still wet and let the leather dry before polishing.
6. In an emergency or when traveling, use a dab of hand lotion to polish leather.

Step Four: Get Out the Stains

1. Go to work on stains as soon as you notice them. The older the stain, the harder it will be to remove. If you cannot deal with a stain right away, seal the shoes in a plastic bag to keep the stain moist until you *can* deal with it.
2. Use alcohol to remove alcohol stains. Coat the whole shoe with alcohol, then let dry and polish.
3. Use rubber cement to get grease and oil out of heavy leather footwear. Brush on small amounts of the rubber cement, let it dry, and rub it off along with the stain.

4. For stained suede, try chalk cleaner, but test it first near the heel.
5. Wash stained fabric uppers on unconstructed shoes, like espadrilles, with soap and water while holding an absorbent cloth inside the shoe. For lined fabric and athletic shoes, use products specifically designed for that footwear.
6. To clean up the damage from winter snow and road salt, wipe leather shoes with a solution of equal parts of warm water and vinegar. Wipe the whole shoe, including heel and sole, let dry, then condition and polish.

Step Five: Dye With Caution

1. Do not try to dye synthetic shoes.
2. If possible, leave the dyeing of leather to professionals. If you must dye shoes yourself, remember that you have to remove the finish on the leather before the color will take to it.
3. Never try to use a light-colored dye on a dark shoe.

Lessons in Lacing
How to Give Your Shoes a Leg Up

Shoes can have multiple lives, given a new twist of their laces. If you have a dowdy pair of sneakers or an old set of oxfords, a new lace or different style of lacing may bring them back into style. Here are suggestions for every old-shoe problem.

Athletic Lacing Chic

CHIC TIP NO. 1: Lace your shoes from the top downward, tying the laces at the toe.

CHIC TIP NO. 2: Use ultrafat laces to fill up the front of the shoe.

CHIC TIP NO. 3: On high-tops, lace up to the ankle, then take the excess of lace and wrap it around the ankle and shoe.

CHIC TIP NO. 4: Tie the laces without a bow, then tuck the ends *inside* the shoe to make your feet look ultracool.

CHIC TIP NO. 5: Use the shoe tongue as a design tool by pulling it up between the laces, then pushing it down and out at the toes. Or pull the tongue in and out between the laces to create a snow-slope effect.

CHIC TIP NO. 6: Double-lace your shoes using two separate laces. Tennis players claim this holds the shoe more tightly closed.

CHIC TIP NO. 7: Double-knot your laces. Tie a bow, then use the bow to tie a bow. It keeps the tie from slipping.

CHIC TIP NO. 8: If you're wearing leather laces, sprinkle the knot with water to hold it tight.

Tie a Satin Ribbon

PARTY TIP NO. 1: Cut satin ribbons the lengths of shoe laces, and use them to tie up children's oxfords for party time.

PARTY TIP NO. 2: Use short lengths of ribbon and tie them at intervals all the way up the front of the shoe to create a flurry of bows.

PARTY TIP NO. 3: Tie solid-color leather shoes with taffeta ribbons, and patterned shoes, with plain satin or grosgrain. Try white satin on children's black patent leathers or pale blue on white patents.

PARTY TIP NO. 4: Color-coordinate shoe ribbons and hair ribbons.

PARTY TIP NO. 5: Use an extra-long ribbon to lace up the shoe, then wrap it around the ankle and tie it in a bow.

PARTY TIP NO. 6: For special occasions, braid colored laces to create a two-toned effect. For Christmas, use red and green, for Easter yellow and lavender, for Valentine's Day red and white.

Rings on Her Fingers and Bells on Her Toes

ACCESSORIZED LACING TIP NO. 1: Lace some bells onto your shoe for fun. It's especially appropriate when Christmas caroling and fun for newly walking toddlers.

ACCESSORIZED LACING TIP NO. 2: Tie on pompoms or feathers for a touch of color.

ACCESSORIZED LACING TIP NO. 3: Use rhinestone shoe clips or satin bows to spruce up black pumps for evening. Try to find shoe clips to match your earrings. Enameled shoe clips in contrasting colors can pick up a solid colored pair of shoes.

ACCESSORIZED LACING TIP NO. 4: Play the colors of laces off colors in socks. For extra fun, layer several pairs of socks in different colors.

It's the Velcro Generation

HI-TECH TIP NO. 1: Shoes with velcro closures can help your child learn to put on shoes, but don't eliminate lace-up shoes entirely, or he or she won't learn to tie a knot or make a bow.

HI-TECH TIP NO. 2: Supervise young children as they put on and take off shoes with velcro. Little children tend to yank off the velcro, rendering the shoes useless.

HI-TECH TIP NO. 3: Don't wear shoes with velcro closures if you're a serious athlete. Velcro loosens with time and tension, making the shoes unstable in heavy-duty wear.

Make the Best of Your Feet

A User's Guide to Foot Care

Leonardo Da Vinci called the human foot "a masterpiece of engineering and a work of art," but feet can't keep on functioning painlessly and looking beautiful without some help from time to time. Their job is to absorb impact, not abuse. The following guidelines for basic foot care will help you keep your feet looking and feeling their best.

1. Wash your feet every day with warm water and soap, then dry them well. Follow this with foot powder to help them stay dry and odor-free. If your feet perspire heavily, consider using an antiperspirant on your soles.
2. Exercise your feet daily with some form of brisk activity, like walking. Make sure to wear appropriate supportive footwear.
3. Put your feet up whenever you can. This helps boost blood circulation.
4. Trim your toenails at least once a week. After bathing, gently push back the cuticles and cut long nails straight

across to prevent ingrown toenails. File rough nails in one direction only to avoid tearing and breaking.

5. Keep the skin on your feet as soft as possible to prevent cracking and the formation of calluses. Use a wet pumice stone to remove dead skin. Massage your feet with hand cream or body lotion after bathing.

6. Check your feet regularly for such problems as corns, bunions, and ingrown nails. If you have any of these problems, consult a podiatrist as soon as possible.

7. Alternate pairs of shoes from one day to the next. Shoes need about a day to dry out thoroughly between wearings. By allowing them to dry thoroughly, you minimize the growth of fungus and foot odor.

8. To ease the strain on your feet and legs, change shoes a couple of times during the day. Every shoe wears differently. By changing styles, you shift pressure points, and your feet won't tire as quickly.

9. Whenever possible, go barefoot on soft surfaces, like sand, lawn, or carpet. This airs your feet and gives them a chance to move and stretch without restraint. On harder surfaces, wear sandals to give your feet the chance to breathe.

10. Wear clean stockings or socks every day. Make sure they're the right size so that they neither bind nor bunch. Avoid garters or hosiery that constricts circulation in your legs.

Special Considerations

Feet may be affected by illness in the rest of the body. Diabetes, arthritis, and circulatory disorders all may show up in the feet. In these cases, the feet require special attention. Herbal powders are available to warm cold feet.

Diabetes

1. Bathe your feet daily and check them for cuts, blisters, corns, etc.
2. Avoid extremes in temperature.
3. Exercise daily.
4. Stay off any foot injury, even if it's painless.
5. Don't soak your feet or use commercial medications on them.
6. Don't wear cutout shoes or sandals.

Circulation Problems or Pregnancy

1. Keep your feet warm.
2. Put a pillow at the foot of the bed to keep the covers off your feet.
3. Consult your doctor if your feet tingle or become numb and blue.
4. Don't stand in one position for extended periods.
5. Never wear garters or restrictive socks.
6. Never apply heat directly to your feet.
7. Don't remove splinters or treat infections without some professional advice.
8. Rotate ankles to improve circulation.
9. Elevate feet periodically.
10. Wear support hose.
11. Try a glass of milk and a banana at night to prevent leg cramps.

Crises and Cures

Symptoms and Treatments for
Common Foot Ailments

"On, my aching feet." If you've never said those words, you're either very young, very sensible about footwear and exercise, or else you're blessed. Twenty percent of children, 80 percent of women, and a substantial percentage of men suffer from foot problems at some point. About 70 percent of all athletic injuries affect the legs and feet. And for more than 4 million Americans, foot problems constitute a major disability.

Some foot problems are symptomatic of more serious diseases, like diabetes, arthritis, cancer, or circulatory disorders. Most, however, are the result of neglect or abuse of your feet. They're easy to prevent and less easy, but not impossible, to reverse. The following crises and cures cover the most common footwear complaints.

CRISIS

ATHLETE'S FOOT
A fungal infection that affects the skin and nails. Itching, scaling, and small blisters are the symptoms. The fungus grows in warm, moist, dark atmospheres, like your shoe.

BUNIONS
Painful inflammation at the base of the big toe that causes the toe to angle, squeezing and overlapping the second toe. Causes may be hereditary, poor posture, or faulty foot structure.

CALLUSES
Hardened patches of skin that occur as protection against friction.

CURE

To prevent athlete's foot, keep your feet clean and dry by changing socks frequently and sprinkling antifungal powder or cornstarch between your toes. If you get athlete's foot, see your podiatrist or doctor. You'll need a prescription medication.

Prevention is far better and simpler than the cure for bunions. Avoid wearing tight shoes that pinch the toes. Once the bunion is established, the only cure is surgery, and that will be effective only if you refrain from tight shoes after the procedure. The surgery itself is unpleasant, but can be performed as an office procedure. The podiatrist makes one or two small incisions in the top or side of the big toe, then inserts a drill to pulverize the bony bump that forms the bunion. After removing the bump, the toe is realigned. After the incisions are stitched, the foot is taped to hold it in the correct position for three weeks.

Calluses usually don't require removal. However, they may become too thick for comfort, or they may be removed for

CRISIS

CURE

cosmetic purposes. To remove a callus, soak it for 10 minutes in warm water, dry, then rub with a moistened pumice stone. To not trim your own calluses if you're diabetic, since you have a heightened risk of infection.

CORNS

A painful, cone-shaped thickening of dead skin with eye, or root, pointing inward. Constant pinching, rubbing, and pressure cause corns.

Corns can be treated at home. First soak the skin, then carefully remove the upper layers with sterilized scissors or a pumic stone. Afterward, protect the area with a non-medicated felt pad with a hole cut in the shape of the corn. Do *not* try to remove the corn at home if you have diabetes, poor circulation, a foot infection, or poor vision. Corns can be treated by a podiatrist.

INGROWN TOENAILS

The side of the nail cuts into the cuticle, resulting in inflammation and possibly infection.

Prevent ingrown toenails by cutting toenails straight across the top. If you feel a toenail starting to imbed itself, soak your foot in warm water, dry it, then gently place a wisp of cotton between the skin and the nail edge. Leave the cotton on for three weeks, until the nail has grown out. In aggravated cases, a slice of nail, or spicule, grows into the toe. It must be removed before healing can occur. Podiatrists remove the nail as a simple office procedure.

CRISIS   **CURE**

PLANTAR WARTS
Benign grows on the bottom
of the foot caused by a virus.
The virus usually is contracted
while stepping on an abrasive
surface, which rubs it into the
skin. If untreated, it can
spread to other parts of your
body.

First have a doctor make sure
the wart is not a corn or other
growth. If it's small, you may
be able to treat it with an over-
the-counter wart remover. If
the wart is well established,
you will need to have your
podiatrist or dermatologist remove it using dry ice, acid, or
some form of surgery.

To Orthotic or Not to Orthotic?
How to Tell the Difference

An orthotic is a shoe insert that helps you walk, run, or stand in
a more comfortable or normal way. Most orthotics are prescribed by podiatrists. Most are custom-formed according to
plaster casts made of the foot. Computer and laboratory analy-
ses may be used to evaluate the effectiveness of an orthotic in
correcting problem foot movement. Because of these elaborate
construction and evaluation processes, orthotics may cost as
much as $400. Others, such as those supplied by Vans for
children, are remarkably inexpensive.

Orthotics fall into three general categories:

1. *Rigid Orthotics* are made out of firm materials, such as
   plastic, metal, or leather. The purpose of most rigid
   orthotics is to control motion in two major foot joints that lie
   below the ankle. They correct the movement of the foot
   and, in some cases, compensate for differences in length
   between one leg and the other.
2. *Soft Orthotics* are made out of soft materials that absorb
   shock. They're designed to improve balance and take pressure off sensitive or sore spots on the sole of the foot. Soft
   orthotics are often prescribed for people with arthritic or

deformed feet who lack adequate fat deposits for cushioning.

3. *Semirigid orthotics* are the inserts most frequently prescribed for athletes. Made from such materials as cork, leather, and synthetics, semirigid orthotics are designed to adjust the movement of the foot to the specific demands of a particular sport.

Do You Need an Orthotic?

You can tell if you need an orthotic by checking your shoes and your body. If you discover the following telltale signals, you may want to visit your podiatrist for further advice.

Physical Signals

1. Low back pain.
2. Leg fatigue.
3. Shooting pains in your calf.
4. Burning sensations in the ball of your foot.
5. Soreness in the middle of your heel.
6. Cramps or aching in the arch of your foot.
7. Pain under the kneecap or in the knee joint.
8. Aching in or around the hip joint.
9. Soreness around the Achilles tendon.
10. Corns or calluses anywhere on your feet.

Footwear Checkpoints

Examine shoes that you've worn regularly for at least two months:

1. Place your shoes on a tabletop and check the inside of the heels for wear. Normally, the outer corners wear down first. If the inner corners are worn, you may be rolling your foot inward, or pronating. This can cause serious knee problems. Orthotics can correct for pronation.
2. Look at the seam that runs vertically down the back, or counter, of the shoe. If it's no longer in a straight vertical line, you may need to correct the movement of your foot.
3. Look at the insole at the ball of the foot. It should show a straight diagonal pattern of wear. If instead the pattern is

circular, you may be rolling off the side of your big toe as you walk. Orthotics can help to balance your weight and prevent this problem.

Tips for Traveling Feet
A Sightseer's Survival Guide

When going on a vacation in the next few weeks, give your feet—and yourself—a break. If you groom your feet for the trip, you'll have a much more active, comfortable, and enjoyable time. Whether your plans include sightseeing on city streets, hiking in the wilderness, or racing from airplane to tour bus, follow these tips.

Before You Leave
Two or three weeks before leaving for vacation, start doing the following exercises and do them every day.

1. Walk barefoot on tiptoe for several minutes.
2. Practice picking up marbles or a pencil with your toes.
3. Wiggle your toes back and forth.
4. Stand on the edge of a bath towel and curl your feet and toes so that they pull in the entire towel.
5. As you stand on the sand or a thick carpet, curl your toes under while keeping your heels on the ground.
6. Use your feet to toss a light ball around the yard or room.
7. Roll your foot over a thick candle or can.
8. Curl your feet in and out, toward each other and away from each other.
9. Rotate your feet from the ankle until your muscles and joints feel stretched and loose.

Packing

1. Avoid shoes with heels, except for special dressy occasions.
2. Don't pack any shoes that you haven't worn for at least one month.
3. Bring comfortable walking shoes with good arch support and a well-padded sole.

4. Bring shoes that are large enough to allow for swelling on airplanes and at the end of strenuous days.
5. Pack plenty of stockings or socks.
6. Pack foot powder and cushioning for emergency relief and comfort.

On Your Trip

1. Scrub your feet—front, back, and between the toes—every day. Use a pumice stone or skin-remover cream if you have dry, scaly patches. Dry your feet well, moisturize, and powder them.
2. Check your feet for trouble signals. Make sure there's no redness or scaly patches between the toes, which could indicate a fungus infection. If you notice the start of a corn, put on a doughnut-shaped piece of moleskin to keep it from being aggravated.
3. Soak your feet at the end of long days.
4. Put your feet up as often as you can on strenuous days.
5. If your feet start to ache and you can't sit down, shift your weight to the outsides of your feet to relieve the pressured points.

The Great American Shoe Stores*
For Connoisseurs Only

The Specialty Stores

For Extravagance

Avventura, Chicago   Soft leathers and high style in footwear for men.

Botticelli, New York   For those who wish to shop in the atmosphere of a "modern ruin."

Walter Chase, San Francisco and other locations   The shoe resource for the career man or woman. Video and events, mixed with personalized service.

*This is a partial list only. Stores are listed alphabetically, not by rating.

Giorgio, Beverly Hills   A celebrity gathering spot in the heart of Rodeo Drive, complete with a bar and pool table.

Goldi's, Milwaukee, Wisconsin   Immaculate and feminine, great private labels.

Parisian, Mobile, Alabama   Fashion entertainment for shoppers via laser discs, video, and direct network transmissions.

Rick Pallack, Sherman Oaks, California   Head-to-toe dressing for the discriminating, cost-conscious man.

The Right Bank, Palm Springs   One-of-a-kind items coupled with fashion flair.

E. J. Robins, Sheepshead Bay, New York   Class fashion in casual surroundings, with an infamous two-for-one sale.

Romanie, St. Louis   In America's heartland, a European boutique with rare imports from Italy.

Roz & Sherm, Detroit, Michigan   Upgraded class with an unusual flair.

Fred Segal, Hollywood and Santa Monica   Trendy clothes for the upwardly mobile, from punk to elegance, men and women alike.

The Shoe and Clothing Connection, Woodland Hills, California   Sumptuous selections sprawl across an entire shopping center of stores.

The Shoe Box, Dallas   Fashion takes on new dimensions in this eight-store chain owned by G. H. Bass.

Timothy's and Timothy Oh!, Fifteen stores in the South and Midwest   For those in the fashion know, a store with variety, drama, and fun.

Veronika's, Cleveland   Housed in an old theater, a boutique that offers ensemble advice and fashion highlights.

Amen Wardy, Newport Beach, California   Created for the wealthy of Southern California, a store with doormen and in-store models.

Wilkes Bashford, San Francisco   Catering to the movers and shakers of northern California, two facing stores for men and women.

The Department Stores

For Pure Chic
Bloomingdale's, *New York*
Henri Bendel, *New York*
Bergdorf Goodman, *New York*
Bonwit Teller, *New York*
I. Magnin, *San Francisco*
Neiman Marcus, *Dallas, Beverly Hills and San Francisco*

For Quality and Quantity
B. Altman & Co., *New York*
Bamberger's, *New Jersey*
Bullock's, *West Coast*
Burdine's, *Miami*
Carson Pierie Scott & Co., *Chicago*
Dayton's, *Minneapolis*
The Emporium, *San Francisco*
Famous Barr, *St. Louis*
Gimbels, *New York*
Kaufmann's, *Pittsburgh*
L. S. Ayres, *Indianapolis*
Lord & Taylor, *New York*
Macy's, *New York and San Francisco*
Marshall Field & Co., *Chicago*
May Company, *Cleveland and West Coast*
Nordstrom's, *Seattle and Southern California*
Robinson's, *Los Angeles*
Saks Fifth Avenue, *New York and Los Angeles*
Stix Baer & Fuller, *St. Louis*

Great Shoe Collections of the World
The Keepers of the Art

The following list includes museums and corporations that have extensive collections of historically interesting footwear.

Museums
Costume Collection, Metropolitan Museum of Art (New York)
Hollywood Museum (Los Angeles)
Guildhall Museum, London Museum, and Victoria and Albert
   Museum (London)
National Museum of Ireland (Dublin)
Charles Jourdan Shoe Museum or Romans-fur-Ilère (Romans,
   France)
Adidas Sports Shoe Museum (Herzogenaurach, West Ger-
   many)
Bally's Museum (Schoenwerd, Switzerland)

Corporate Collections
Bata Shoe Collection (Montreal, Canada)
Presidential Shoe Collection, Genesco, Inc. (Nashville, Ten-
   nessee)
Kinney Shoe Collection (New York, New York)
Thom McAn Historical Shoe, Thom McAn Shoe Company
   (Worcester, Massachusetts) Collection